ROCK SOLID

A Very Good Life

To: Candace
"From my heart"
Bob C

ROCK SOLID
A Very Good Life

Bob Kreilick

Bardolf & Company Sarasota 2010

Published by Bardolf & Company

ROCK SOLID
A Very Good Life

ISBN 978-0-9841745-4-6

Copyright © 2010 by Bob Kreilick
All rights reserved.

No part of this book may be used or reproduced in any manner whatsoever without written permission except in the case of brief quotations embodied in critical articles and reviews.

For information, address and editorial inquiries, please contact
  Bardolf & Company
  5430 Colewood Pl
  Sarasota, FL 34232
  tel. 941-232-0113

Library of Congress Cataloging-in-Publication Data
has been applied for.

First edition

Cover and layout by Shaw Creative
www.shawcreativegroup.com

Printed in the United States

To Barbara
the wind beneath my wings

INTRODUCTION

I never thought my life was anything special or worth writing about. Although I've spent a good seven decades on this planet, I can't say that anything out of the ordinary has happened to me. Except for my wife, Barbara, dying of a brain aneurysm seven years ago, there haven't been any tragedies in my life. I haven't been a hero—rescuing people from the jaws of death, or a star athlete, or a famous entertainer or singer. In fact, there are some people who would probably pay good money for me not to sing in public. Nothing I've ever done is going to get me into the *Guinness Book of Records*. I can't imagine anyone naming a building or street or park after me.

Yet when I've gotten together with my friends and swapped stories about our lives, many times they've told me, "You really should write a book."

So a year ago, I decided to take them up on their challenge, and the book you're holding in your hands is the result of my efforts. I've written it from the heart and hope you'll enjoy it.

If I've learned anything from this, it's that what matters are the people in my life—my good friends, my family growing up, and my children. I have been blessed with all of them.

Bob Krcilick
Sarasota, Florida, 2010

Chapter 1
SCRANTON

I was born on May 17, 1938, in a three-story house on Wheeler Avenue in the Petersburg section of East Scranton, Pennsylvania. My parents moved a lot—we probably lived in six different locations during the time I grew up there, but I spent most of my early life on Myrtle Street next to the Petersburg Silk Mill. Scranton was still a bustling town then because of its anthracite coal mines, textile factories and long-time connection with the railways and steel industries in the Lackawanna River Valley that included the cities of Wilkes-Barre, Pittston and Carbondale. But some of the sheen of Scranton's former glory, when it was named The Electric City because it had the first successfully operating electric streetcar system in the United States, was wearing thin. (Nowadays, Scranton is best known for being birthplace of the current vice president of the United States, Joe Biden, and for serving as the location for the hit television series "The Office.")

When I was young, the Laurel Line, which opened in 1905, still ran past Myrtle and James Streets up into Dunmore, the suburb of East Scranton where the Erie Pennsylvania Railroad had its car shops. It was actually a tram that had a third rail like a subway, and it went all the way from Scranton to Wilkes Barre. The third rail carried high voltage, and as children we were warned not to go near it. If, during one of our games, a ball ended up close to it, we made no effort to retrieve it and just left it there. Although a number of animals—cats, dogs, squirrels and raccoons—were electrocuted from time to time, to my knowledge no person was ever hurt.

We lived near a culm dump—that's what they call the waste heaps from the coal mines—and I can still remember the fires that started there at night from spontaneous combustion. In those days, they let them burn and I could see them from my bedroom window across the baseball field next to the silk mill. (Nowadays, they drill holes into the mounts and fill them with water to put out the fires.)

Many of the women in the neighborhood worked at the Petersburg Silk Mill and fabric mills in other parts of the town, although my mom didn't. She had a job in the medical records department of the nearby Hahnemann Hospital, which is now called the Community Medical Center.

Our house was also close to the Delaware, Lackawanna and Western Railroad tracks, and a couple of times a day the trains coming through would blow their whistle before and after going through a tunnel on the way to the Scranton station. I loved the sound of the trains, the chugging of the steam engines, the clackety-clack of the cars riding over the railroad ties. When the wind came from the east, the smell of sulfur permeated the air, and everything was blackened with soot—the red bricks of the silk factory, the baseball field next to it where we played ball, the roofs on the houses in the neighborhood, and even the leaves on the trees.

I grew up as middle child of three brothers. Bill was four years older than me and Charles—we called him Butch—was four years younger. I had an older sister, Janet, but she died of appendicitis before I was born. She was three years old, and by the time my parents took her to the hospital because she wouldn't stop crying, it was too late.

I'm told that my dad was beside himself. He vented his fury on the doctors and got so mad he wanted to choke somebody, but it really wasn't anyone's fault. It did make him change jobs, though. He'd been a Pennsylvania state trooper, patrolling the highways on an Indian motorcycle. In his leather uniform—cap, spit-shiny leather jacket and belt, and boot leggings—he cut a dashing figure. He was one of three motorcycle cops known to be tough, and nobody messed around with them.

My father in uniform in front of the Berwick, PA, police station.

By the time I was old enough to understand about his former career, he hadn't been a cop for some years, but I still heard stories about him tracking down criminals and arresting them. One time in winter he chased a speeder on his motorcycle. The road was covered with ice, and taking a turn at a steep angle, he put his knee down to brace himself and all but sheared off his kneecap. Fortunately, it didn't cause any permanent damage, and he soon returned to duty.

In those days, state troopers had to live away from home in the barracks, which were in Berwick, Pennsylvania, when they were working. They even had had to apply for permission to get married. I still have the consent letter from my father's highway patrol troop major, granting approval to my parents' wedding.

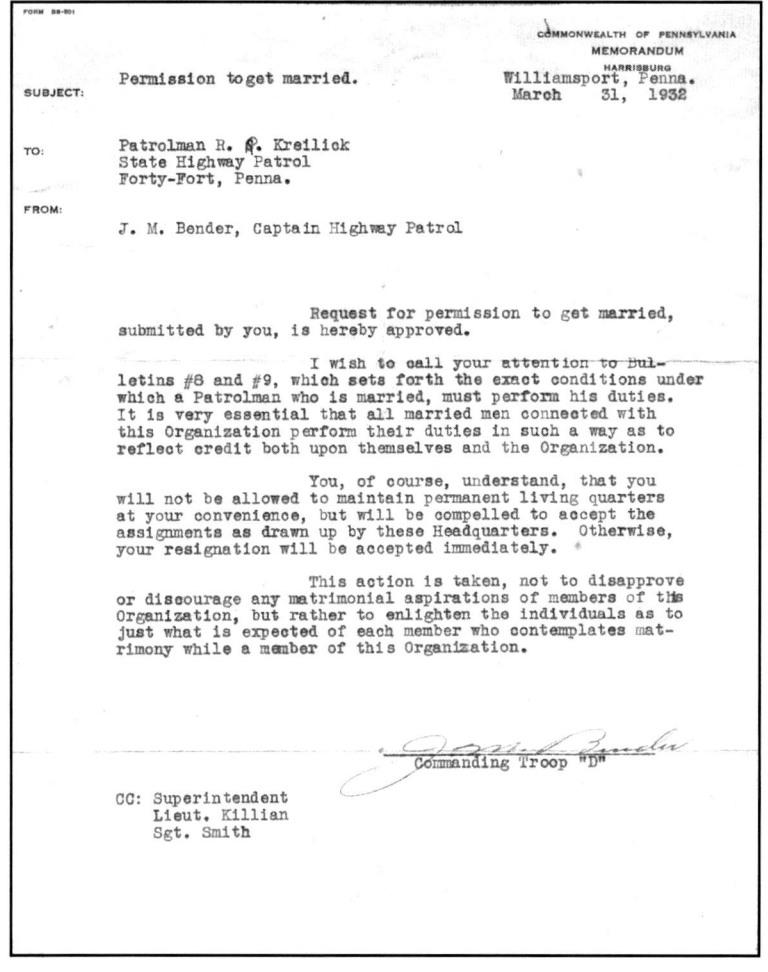

The relevant lines read,

> You, of course, understand that you will not be allowed to maintain permanent living quarters at your convenience, but will be compelled to accept the assignments as drawn up by these Headquarters.

My dad got married, but he hated to be away from my mother and sister; and while he loved his job, he loved his family more. So he quit.

My father, mother, brother Bill and me.

For a while he worked as a detective for the Bethlehem Steel Company, but he ended up spending most of his work life in the car shop of the Erie Railroad in Dunmore, a suburb of Scranton, fixing railroad cars. In between times, he drove a truck for Burschel

Dairy (I still have a milk bottle he delivered), tended bar, and later was my helper from time to time on my jobs as a driller.

My dad was a loving father. He came to all of my football games in high school and did the same for my brother Butch later on. He was also one of toughest guys I knew, strong as a bull and good with his hands. He was just over 6 feet tall and weighed around 210 pounds. Although he had a German background, he was not temperamental or especially stubborn, but he had a reputation in the neighborhood of never backing down from anyone.

A typical story about him went like this: One night when he tended bar, a kid from the neighborhood who'd been in the Marines came in. His name was Donnie Schmidt. He was in his early 20s and thought he was tough as nails. After a few drinks, he said to my dad, "You know, Ray, I know you've got a reputation as a tough guy, but I think I can take you."

My dad said, "Donnie, you've had a few drinks, but calm down or I'll have to shut you off and send you home."

Well, Donnie kept at him, so finally my dad leapt over the bar and knocked the daylights out of him.

Donnie went slinking home, got his father, Harold, and together they came back. The bar went silent anticipating another big fight.

First thing out of my dad's mouth was, "Harold, he was acting up. I had to throw him out. And if you want some of the same, come and get it."

Harold put up one hand in surrender and said, "No, Ray, I just wanted to hear what happened. I'm not looking for any trouble."

And he turned around and walked out with Donnie in tow.

But that wasn't the end of it. An hour later, the kid came back alone, walked up to my dad and said, "Ray, you got me once, but I don't think you can do it again."

My dad didn't smile. He just looked at him and said in a quiet voice, "Donnie, I'll take you to the Erie car shop where nobody can hear you scream, and I'm going to beat the living shit out of you."

And that was that. Donnie wanted no more of my dad.

Donnie wasn't a bad guy. He was just feeling his oats, coming out of the Marine Corps. Later on, he had a place near the hunting camp my dad built with some of his friends in 1943 in Pike County, close to New York by the Delaware River, and he'd come down when he knew we had a meeting. No hard feelings.

Some of my earliest memories stem from spending time at the hunting camp, which was called the East Scranton Sportsmen's Club. My father took me along from age 3 on, and I still remember sitting in the deer stand on bitter cold mornings, bundled up in sweaters and overcoat, shivering and watching my breath turn white.

During the summer, we'd also go up there and fish for smallmouthed bass, blue gills and eels on the Delaware River. My mom and dad never took a vacation. Spending a weekend up by the camp was the closest they ever came to doing so.

As I got older, I always liked to hear the story of how the camp had come about. Apparently, the previous owner had gone a bit mad and had set fire to his house. Two members of the Cortese family, who owned a lot of property in the area, happened to come by on horseback, and when they rode up to the burning building to see what was happening, he shot them dead and then killed himself. By the time the conflagration had died down, all that was left of the place was the foundation. When the family put the property up for sale, my dad and his friends saw the ad in the paper, checked the place out and bought it, 190 acres in all. They built the lodge on the original foundation. It's a cozy two-story building with a large common room and kitchen on the ground floor. The upstairs bedrooms sleep 17 men.

When I was young, I sometimes wondered if the ghost of the crazy owner haunted the place, but if he did, he must have turned friendly because nothing bad ever happened there since. On the contrary, over the course of the 55 years that I have been a member (I took my brother Bill's place when he went into the Marines), I have spent many wonderful times there, and I still go up to meetings and for hunting season whenever I can.

Another example of my dad's toughness occurred after I finished high school, when my brother Bill came home for a visit. He went out partying to a tavern in the Pocono Mountains with my mom and dad and one of their friends, Spike Winters, who drove a tanker for Texaco. After a few drinks they all went outside and watched as my dad and Spike tossed firecrackers from the front porch.

The town bully took offense and came over. He said, "What are you doing? You're making too much noise!"

My mom tried to make light of it. "Aw, we're just having fun."

The bully would have none of it. He pushed my mother and punched Bill, knocking him backwards over the hood of a car.

When my dad saw that, he chased the guy down, tackled him and knocked just about every tooth out of his mouth, putting him in the hospital.

In the process, my dad broke his hand. When I got up the next morning and came down to breakfast at our house, my dad's hand was in a plaster cast.

I asked, "What happened?"

He shrugged and said, "Oh, we had a little altercation."

It was Bill who told me later on with considerable pride what had happened. My dad would never blow his own horn.

My dad was working at the Erie Railroad car shop in Dunmore by then, and he never lost a day's work. He wielded hammers and wrenches and screwdrivers with his hand in a cast, like it was nothing at all.

I don't want you to think that my dad was a bruiser. He never looked for trouble and didn't brag about himself. But in the rough-and-tumble world of working class Scranton, he knew how to take care of himself, and if anyone messed with his family, heaven help him.

My parents, Bill and me.

My mother, whose maiden name was Margaret Montgomery, was a great mom. She was born in Glasgow, Scotland, and she was 3 years old when her parents immigrated to the United States. Although we didn't have a lot of money (there were times when my parents had food stamps), she never succumbed to the penny-pinching quality that Scots are reputed to have. She made sure we always had a buck in our pocket when we went to school and clothes on our backs. Although we weren't the fanciest dressed, we were always neat and clean. My pants, shirts and socks had been darned numerous times, because they were hand-me-downs from my brother Bill. By the time I got his sneakers, the KEDS logo on the circular ankle patch was half worn away. By the time my brother Butch got them, there was no lettering at all.

My mom on the backwall at 2117 Myrtle Street.

My mom worked every day and cooked for us when she came home at night. I can still remember the taste of her meatloaf and mashed potatoes—we had meatloaf a lot. She was great with pies and dumplings, too. All good, old-fashioned, meat-on-the-ribs meals.

When I grew up, our neighborhood was a real melting pot. There were Germans, Poles and Irish living right next to one another, and the Bunker Hill section right next to Petersburg was home to many Italian families. I still remember the heavy-set Italian woman who would come walking down from Matthew Avenue with a great big tub on her head, calling out, "Huckelabellies, huckelabellies," peddling the berries she'd picked in the nearby woods. Everyone called her Huckleberry Mary.

Some of the melting pot atmosphere literally rubbed off on Mom's cooking—Friday was always spaghetti night. And on Good Friday, we always had noodles and prunes. I don't know if that was a German tradition or just unique to our family.

In fact, people's cooking and food preparation created odors that always wafted through the the air in our neighborhood. All the women baked their own bread. And all the Italian guys produced homemade wine. When I was peddling newspapers in high school, I could smell the wine as I went by their houses, and I would detect the aroma of Mrs. Rizzo's famous pasta with sausage, peppers and onions from a block away. If you went inside her house, you'd get knocked over by it.

All the families had gardens and grew their own onions, carrots, horseradish and rhubarb. I can still remember my mother-in-law grating the horseradish on her back porch, tears streaming down her cheeks. My dad would cook the rhubarb into a tasty stew for dessert. He'd cut off the leaves and the bottom off the stalks, chop what was left into little pieces, throw them in a pot with water and sugar, and boil it all down. My mouth still waters just thinking about it.

From time to time we also had pheasant, rabbit or venison we brought home from the hunting camp. One of my dad's cousins had a butcher shop on Ash Street, and we'd take the deer there on our way home. He'd butcher it for us and package it up. We'd split it up among the different members of the camp and keep it frozen at home for special occasions.

Our neighborhood was a real community. Everybody knew everybody and looked out for one another. People never locked their doors. For us kids, it was a great place to grow up. No one minded us, and we'd play from after school until evening, until my dad would whistle—time to come home. Those days are gone now.

Another example of how things were then, perhaps for the better: One of my father's sisters, my aunt Ruth, worked as an elevator operator for *The Scranton Times* in the downtown headquarters. It was one of those old-fashioned cages with a metal gate that slid across the opening and an operating handle that moved in a half circle. She knew everyone that worked in the building, and they knew her. The company kept her on the job until she retired, even though it could have replaced her with an automatic elevator years earlier. Only the day after her retirement dinner did they inaugurate the new one with push buttons for the passengers.

My best friend, Billy Hoffman, lived around the corner from us on James Street. I've known him since we were 3 years old. Although he was an only child, he had a large extended family of uncles and aunts. I spent a lot of time at his house. Billy's dad, Harry, drove a panel truck for the Cook Coffee Company, and it was a shame that he died at a relatively young age. His mom, Sue, worked at the Petersburg Silk Mill, and I still think of her as my second mom. She still lives near Scranton, in Dunmore, at Maywood College, an assisted living facility; and, at age 93, her mind is sharp as a tack.

Billy and I went to kindergarten, grade school and high school together. He was the quarterback on the Scranton Tech football team and a terrific baseball player—he played third base and shortstop for most of his career. I consider Billy one of the 10 most talented athletes that ever came out of Scranton. He could have been a major leaguer in baseball for sure. After high school, when he went on to Indiana University of Pennsylvania, he was the school's starting quarterback and played baseball.

In 2008, he was inducted into the school's Hall of Fame, and I am proud to have been there for that. He lives around the corner from me now, in Sarasota, that's how close we've been for nearly 70 years!

We had quite a neighborhood gang, all going to the same grade schools: Muhlenberg School #5 from kindergarten to 3rd grade, then William Prescott Elementary School through 8th grade. The core members were Billy and I, and Steve Wojdak, who was blond and Polish and also a good athlete. He ended up going to Central High and played quarterback against us. I spent a lot of time at his house, too. He had the nicest parents you could find. His uncle, Will Magnotta, was quite short and everyone called him by his nickname, Peanuts.

Steve later became an important attorney and lobbyist in Philadelphia, and he was later indicted and convicted for bribery and fraud. His firm is well-known and he has had his hands in local politics for many years. He is the only one of the gang that hasn't stayed in touch. After he left Scranton for good, I never heard from him again.

But at the time, Billy, Steve and I were like the three musketeers, with the others on the side. There was Joe Pacifico, who lived on Richter Avenue, which ran along the Roaring Brook. He wasn't an athlete, but he had a great, outgoing personality. Then there was Billy Hill, the toughie in the neighborhood who later went to prison—word on the street was that he murdered someone. And Carmen Castelano and Billy Bronson, another toughie. I don't know what happened to them.

William Prescott #38 Elementary School: I am in the top row, far left. Billy Hoffman is in the black shirt. Third row from the top: Steve Wojdak, fifth from left; Joe Pacifico, third from left.

Across the street from Billy lived the Foytacks. They were a large family and all the boys were good athletes. Paul Foytack, who was eight years older than us, was the most talented and ended up pitching for the Detroit Tigers from 1957 to 1964.

Another family of good athletes on James Avenue were the Rozelles. Ken Rozelle, who was my brother Bill's age, became a good friend later on. He was very goodlooking. I remember him as a hero-athlete in the neighborhood as I grew up. He was one of the best football running backs to come out of Scranton Tech High School, and we all looked up to him. He also had two sisters, Gail and JoAnn—great gals. JoAnn was the older of the two. She looked like Jane Russell, the movie star, and had all of us youngsters daydreaming as we got older.

After school we'd play on the baseball field next to the Petersburg Silk Mill. Or we'd head to Nay Aug Park, just a few blocks away. It was a huge public park that had been designed by Frederick Law Olmsted, the architect of New York City's Central Park. It was big enough to get lost in, with beautifully sculpted woodsy hills and meadows, and we knew every inch of it like the back of our hands. There was the Everhart Museum of Natural History, Science and Art on the grounds that had all kinds of stuffed animals and birds—it started out as a collection of creatures native to Pennsylvania, but soon became one of the most extensive in the United States.

The Nay Aug Park Zoo sported tigers, lions, monkeys, Joshua the donkey and Tilly the elephant. Pete Barbutti, a comedian who went to Scranton Tech High School a couple of years before us, once quipped that Nay Aug Park is where old elephants go to die. He became a lounge entertainer in Las Vegas and used to do a number of piano-based gags, such as playing the keys with his nose, "tuning" the piano stool, and using a plumber's helper stuck to the side as a cigar holder. He appeared on the Johnny Carson and Ed Sullivan shows.

In the middle of the park was Lake Lincoln, a big man-made pond lined with concrete, which is now two Olympic-size public swimming pools. In those days, it was surrounded by sidewalks and metal barriers with signs that said, "No Diving. Do Not Dive Over the Bars." But there were always some show-offs—not me, of course—who'd dive over the bars into the shallow, 3-foot deep water. They'd do it on a dare or for cigarettes. One of them was an Italian kid from Bunker Hill. Everyone called him Mostie, but his real name was Longo, and he was older than us. If you saw him come up on one side of the street, you got out of the way and crossed to the other side. You never knew what he'd do to you.

When we wanted to go swimming, we'd head to Little Rocky Glen, a creek outside of town, or go to the waterfall in Nay Aug Park where the Roaring Brook came through. The falls dropped 30 to 40 feet into a scenic gorge that had ledges at different heights both above and below water level. We'd jump or dive off the ones on the walls of the gorge. We even had names for them—The Chair at 20 feet, and The Cable, 60 feet up. It was a lot of fun, but you had to know what you were doing. Some of the kids from Southside or North Scranton, who came to sunbathe and show off for their girls, didn't know where the danger was. Once Billy and I watched as the fire department pulled a couple of kids out of the water who had drowned. They weren't from our neighborhood and they probably got knocked unconscious when they dove in. No one from our neighborhood ever got in trouble there—we knew were all the ledges were.

There also was a bridge high up over the gorge. A couple of people jumped off it to commit suicide, so the park rangers put up a 10-foot-high fence. But before that happened, someone bet Mostie that he wouldn't jump off the bridge into the water below, and he climbed up on the low railing and stood there for some time, poised to leap. His friends begged him not to do it because he'd kill himself, and to everyone's relief, he finally listened and backed off.

As kids, we spent as much time outside as we could. Sometimes, we'd go to the spring by the railroad tracks where the hobos congregated. They'd make a table out of a rock outcropping and play pinochle and poker. It was right near the tunnel where the trains had to slow down, which made it easy for them to get on and off when they were traveling.

They were a rough and ragged bunch, but we never had any trouble because we had Joe Foytack look out for us. Joe had been a professional boxer—he'd fought under the name of Joe O'Neill and had even had a bout at Madison Square Garden in New York—but he'd become punch-drunk. He walked around the neighborhood and smiled and waved to everyone he met. He was a good 20 years older than us, but even though we were just 10, he always called me "Mister Kreilick" and Billy, "Mr. Hoffman." But when we went down to the spring and he'd be there watching the hobos play cards, he'd tell them, "You don't go near these kids. They are my boys."

Although winters in Scranton were bitter cold, it never stopped us. We bundled up and played outside as always. We wore black rubber galoshes—Four-Buckle Arctics that were lined with felt, big enough to fit shoes inside. We also used them as our hunting boots with no shoes, just heavy socks and felt inserts inside. My dad and his friends wore them that way, too. For hats, we had ear loggers with furry flaps that covered the side of our faces. You don't see them much nowadays—only in Elmer Fudd cartoons and in movies with Russian commissars—although my son, Bobby, still has one.

In any case, well outfitted and fortified, we'd go sledding. The hills in our neighborhood and Nay Aug Park made for perfect runs. Most days we'd head up to Lake Lincoln to ice skate. Billy and Steve Wojdak were demon speedsters and raced a lot. They wore the special long-bladed skates. I wasn't that fast and I had ice hockey skates, but I could get around just fine.

My dad ice fishing on Lake Wallenpaupack.

When it snowed, we always made a little extra money shoveling sidewalks and driveways. We made snowmen in the front yards and had epic snowball fights around the neighborhood. We weren't supposed to do that at school, but we'd do it anyway. When we were caught throwing snowballs in the schoolyard at Prescott Elementary, we'd get sent to the office and had to face the principal, Mr. Howard, a tall, handsome, burly man and a fierce disciplinarian.

He'd say, "Hold out your hands. Were you throwing snowballs?"

We'd put out our hands, palms up and knowing what was coming, say, "Yes," and brace ourselves.

WHACK. WHACK.

He'd hit us two or three times with a ruler on each hand. You tell me that didn't sting! Our hands were red and swollen from the cold already because we didn't wear any gloves, and now they really puffed up. He couldn't get away with that today, but those were different times.

For a while, my parents were the caretakers for a summer camp called Moser's Landing on Lake Wallenpaupack about 25 miles east of Scranton. There were eight to 10 cabins and my mother was responsible for their upkeep, while my dad ran the store selling milk, cigarettes, candy and ice. It was an easy way to provide us with a summer vacation while making a little extra money.

By then my brother Bill was in high school, I was in grade school, and Butch had just entered the education system. There were a lot of kids, and we spent all the time in the woods or swimming in the lake. It was a mixed-age crew that included Bill and his friends, as well as grade school kids my age, and Butch.

Whenever we were ready to head down to the lake, my mom and dad would say, "Now you watch your brother."

And we'd promise, "Sure."

When we got there, Bill and I could swim like fish, but Butch was still learning, so my mom had him wear one of those plastic tubes with a duck sticking up at the front. There was a 20-foot cliff on one side of the lake, and we'd jump off it and cannonball into the water. Butch would be watching us from up on top. Pretty soon, Bill and I got the bright idea of throwing him off the cliff.

He'd sail down and hit the water with a big splash and disappear. After a while, the tube would bob up—but no Butch. Before we got worried, though, he'd pop out of the water, gasping for air. One of us or the gang was always there to grab him and make sure he was okay. And Butch loved it. He'd be laughing and begging us, "Throw me off again!"

Everything went smoothly until my dad got wind of what we were doing. He never hit us when we misbehaved, but sometimes he'd give us a kick in the pants. All we had to do was look at him, and we knew we were in trouble. That time with Butch was one of the few occasions we got our behinds kicked.

Another time, we found a great big wooden plank on the water, and we put Butch on it and pushed him out into the lake. He was having a great time dog-paddling around as if he were on a surfboard going out to sea. Unfortunately, just then my dad came down the road to the lake.

He looked around and asked, "Where's your brother?"

We pointed guiltily out to the lake, "That's him out there on the plank."

Well, we got our behinds kicked for that prank, too.

Sometimes I think Butch must have nine lives. One night when my mom and dad went out, we put him on Bill's shoulders and horsed around. But when Bill lost his balance, Butch fell off and hit his head on a corner of the couch. He was lying on the floor, shaking in spasms and his eyes were rolling up in his head. We were mortified and had no idea what to do. You can imagine how relieved we felt when he finally came around. By the time my parents got home, he was fine, though we did make him go to bed.

When they asked, "How's your brother?" we were cool as cucumbers.

"Oh, everything is great!"

Then there were the times when we put Butch on Bob Harvey's shoulders and chased after them around the neighborhood, 10 to 12 kids in their wake. Bob was a boxer and in such good shape that none of our gang could catch them. But things often got out of hand. Once Bob and Butch tumbled down a flight of stairs together and nearly got killed. Another time, Butch caught his neck on the clothesline in a neighbor's yard, which spun him around and plopped him down to the ground. We all ran up and grabbed and shook him, glad that he was all right.

Butch was a gamer. And living up to his nickname as one tough little guy!

Nine lives, I swear.

My brother Bill, me and Butch on the porch at 2117 Myrtle Street.

Butch turned out to be one of the better athletes in the town and clearly the best in our family. As a teenager, he could hit a softball over the railroad tracks at the field by the Petersburg Silk Mill. After high school, when he went to Lycoming College in Williamsport, he was the first freshman to play halfback and end both on offense and defense for the football team. He could do anything with a ball—he was a good football player and a very good baseball player—and he continued to whack softballs over the fence for many years after college. By then he was playing for Middlesex, New Jersey, and lived next door to Charlie Weiss, the college and pro football coach.

In the meantime, our crew continued to have a lot of fun. By the time I was in 6th or 7th grade, we had a club in the garage in the back of the yard and an old car that didn't run. Bob Harvey was the leader of the gang. We'd push that old clunker up a back alley for three to four blocks. Then we'd all pile in and shoot down the alley, crossing the streets, down the hill and whip it into the garage. In between times, we made "Wildcat Goulash" with baked beans and scrambled eggs we confiscated from our families.

By then we had moved to a house on Prescott Avenue. An electric tram ran in the middle of the roadway all the way to the top of the hill, where there was a turnaround, and back down to Mulberry Street where it curved and headed into Scranton. We were nimble youngsters, and rather than pay the fare, we'd jump on the back end and hang on, getting a free ride to the downtown theaters, shops and eating places. When we had nothing better to do, we'd try to pull the couplings from the wires overhead, which would stop the trams cold. (Well, others did that, not me.)

On Saturday afternoons, we'd go to the movies at the Bell Theater. The tickets for the matinees cost 12 cents. They'd always show previews, a newsreel in black-and-white, a cartoon or two, and a serial that ended with a cliff-hanger, and you had to wait until the following week to find out how the hero or heroine survived jumping out of a car or dangling from a rope over a lion pit. Finally came the main feature, usually a cowboy movie starring Roy Rogers, Hopalong Cassidy or Gene Autry. Later on, John Wayne became a special hero of mine—a rock-solid man always true to his word. Whenever we could, we'd spend a couple of pennies for some candy. As we got older, we'd go there to neck and make out with the girls. The Bell Theater was a big part of growing up.

One year—I don't remember which—I gave a girl a black cricket as a present. I handed it to her like a friend. Her name was Judy Knauer, and she ended up becoming a doctor. Nothing ever came of it with her, but from then on my friends started to call me Crick. The nickname stuck with me through grade school and high school. In fact, I think that's the name in my senior yearbook. Billy Hoffman still calls me Crick once in a while, but after I graduated from high school and moved away, it gradually died out.

When my brother Bill turned 17, he got permission from my parents to drop out of high school and join the Marine Corps. He had not been a good student until then, although the military changed that. He finished his high school education and later earned a college degree from East Stroudsburg University in Pennsylvania.

But first he went to Parris Island, South Carolina, for basic training, and shortly after that he got shipped out to Korea.

I was too young to understand much of what went on during World War II. I knew that Billy Hoffman's dad had served, and that Elmer Hawk, the candy maker, had been in Stalag 17, the notorious Nazi prison camp. Elmer was honored when he returned home in a special ceremony held in one of the theaters downtown. But hearing about them hadn't made much of an impression on me. By the time my brother went overseas, I was 13 and had some idea of what it meant to fight. Other than my father, my brother Bill was my first hero. Of course, I had athlete heroes, baseball and football stars like Mickey Mantle of the New York Yankees and Jim Taylor, running back for the Green Bay Packers. But Bill was a hero in the neighborhood for going off to war and fighting America's enemies.

Bill with Grandma Scanlon, our next door neighbor on Myrtle Street, during a visit home.

Still, it was a difficult time for our family the morning two representatives from the Marines came to our house and delivered a telegram that Bill had been wounded in combat. I was in school at the time and got called out of class and taken to the principal. He told me what had happened and sent me home for the day.

The story we got was that Bill had been on a nighttime patrol when he and his fellow Marines were ambushed by a detachment of North Korean soldiers. Bill managed to kill one of them, but there were too many and in the firefight, all his buddies were killed. Bill ended up lying in a rice paddy all night with a wound in his leg. The following morning he was found and airlifted to safety. He spent time on a hospital ship in Incheon Harbor and has a Purple Heart and a six-inch scar on his leg as a testament to his valor. There was also a story in *The Scranton Times* after we received a letter from him, with the headline "Local Marine Gets a Goonie in Korea, Leg Wound Fighting Out of Ambush" nd details of his exploits.

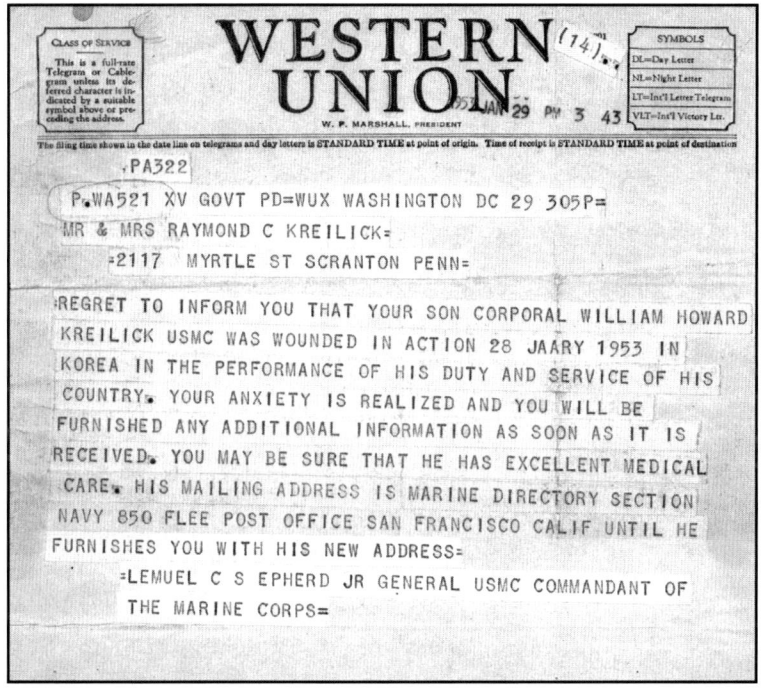

After Bill recovered, he didn't get sent home. He went back and completed two tours in Korea. When he finally came home for good, he gave me his overcoat, shirt, pants and boots, and I was proud to wear them. He was lucky that he healed completely from his wound. I remember Walter Nickelson, another Korean War veteran from Scranton, walking down Myrtle Street awkwardly swinging his arm and dragging his leg behind him.

In the fall of 1955, Bill got married. We played football that Saturday against Clarks Summit and won. After the game, the whole team signed a football to present to him. Then we all piled into cars and drove up to the ceremony at Lake Ariel, and I was the best man!

Bill with my mom and dad on a visit home.

During the 1960s, Bill put in two tours in Vietnam, but by then he was with Intelligence with the First Marine Division, so he wasn't involved in direct combat on the front lines.

Bill served for 20 years in the Marine Corps, including time on three aircraft carriers: the Leyte, the Antietam and the Saratoga. He retired at age 37 as a Master Sergeant, the highest rank one can achieve as a noncommissioned officer. We went with two carloads of friends to Pensacola, Florida, where he was stationed, and saw him being presented with the American flag that had flown over the base and a beautiful sword. It was a very emotional ceremony.

Needless to say, I am very proud of my brother. He is a real hero.

From left to right: My Grandfather Holder, my dad, my brother Bill and Grandfather Charles Kreilick.

Chapter 2
HIGH SCHOOL

When it was time to go to high school, I and all of my friends from the neighborhood went to Scranton Tech, except for Steve Wojdak, who went to Central High.

By then we lived on Gibson Street, and the school was about a mile downhill from my house on the corner of Adams Avenue. Next door to us lived the high school principal, Mr. Murphy, a short, pudgy fellow. When I played varsity football, he often gave me a ride to school in the morning. I'd get out on the front porch and he'd be waiting in his car, waving me over. He came to all the games, and we'd talk about the team and the opponents we'd be facing on the coming weekend.

When I graduated, the tradition continued with Butch, who took over my number 22 football jersey and often got a ride to school with Mr. Murphy.

I was always looking for ways to make a little extra money.

For nearly two years, Billy Hoffman and I delivered newspapers. Billy had the morning route for *The Scranton Tribune,* and I delivered *The Scranton Times* in the evening. Because he had to get up at 5 a.m., his mother drove him in their car. I had to walk. Since I had the biggest route in East Scranton, with 160 customers, I couldn't do it by bike. I'd pick up the papers at the office on Ash Street right next to my old grade school, Muehlenberg #5, in two big, white canvas bags with big white straps. You had to be big—or dumb enough—to carry them, especially on Thursdays when the paper was thick with extra ads and special offers.

I'd roll and fold the papers on the way down the long hill to my first customer. By the time I got to where Mr. Cerato had driven into the railroad bridge and killed himself, I had them all done.

I always felt a little eerie passing that spot, because Mr. Cerato's suicide was one of the most bizarre occurrences in our neighborhood. It had happened fairly recently and had everyone talking. He was a licensed dynamiter in the mines. One afternoon, he'd been sitting across from my dad in Magnotta's Bar on the corner of Ash Street and Wheeler Avenue, where people went after work for a shot and a beer.

He'd looked over and said, "Ray, I'm going to kill myself. I'm tired of living, and I'm going to end it right now."

Then he got off his stool, headed outside, jumped into his car and took off. My dad ran after him and tried to stop him, but he couldn't catch up with him. At the bottom of Ash Street there was a concrete railroad viaduct, and Mr. Cerato crashed head-on into the center pillar with my dad right behind him. Until then he had been, as far as everyone knew, happily married with a couple of kids, and none of us ever figured out what had driven him to such a terrible, self-destructive end. It remained a mystery.

In any case, at that point I had my papers ready to fling on porches, lawns or driveways I knew where to throw them from early on. If you got yelled at, you quickly got the idea where they wanted you to toss them. From there, I'd head up Matthew Avenue through Bunker Hill and end up coming down Myrtle Street to my house. I'd start at 4:30 and get done a couple of hours later. It was a seven-day workweek, and on Sundays we had to go around and collect. We got two cents per paper, and tips on holidays. I gave all my earnings to my mom, and she'd give me a couple of dollars back, so I always had money in my pocket.

My dog used to come with me. His name was Prince and he was a mix of German Shepherd and Terrier. When he ran ahead, people would see him coming and call him—they knew I was right behind. They'd give him a bone or treat. He knew everybody.

Prince used to disappear periodically. He'd be gone two or three days, but we didn't worry. We knew he was roaming the neighborhood, visiting his girlfriends, and that he'd be back. In those days you could let dogs run free. From time to time, we'd get a call from the Nay Aug Zoo—the keepers there knew my mom and dad by name. They'd say, "Mr. Kreilick, Prince is here." So my dad would jump in the car and pick him up.

For a while, after I got my driver's license, I sold ice cream and candy for Elmer Hawk's mother, Gertrude. She had started a candy company in Dunmore. Since its modest beginnings, it has become quite successful and is well known as Gertrude Hawk Chocolates. I drove a little, motorized truck with a freezer all over Bunker Hill and Petersburg. It didn't have one of those hurdy-gurdy musical themes like "Pop Goes the Weasel" to announce my arrival, but when I blew my horn, the kids knew I was coming and lined up on the sidewalk with their pennies, eager for a special treat. I did it for about nine months in the afternoons after school, during the off-season when it didn't interfere with football practice.

After I got my driver's license, I also started my own business. I had a card printed up for "Bob's Super Service—Service with a Smile" offering to wash cars and repair their brakes. I still have the card.

Neither of my parents were especially religious. I started off as a Presbyterian when I was young and my mom and dad attended Westminster Presbyterian Church in downtown Scranton. I went with them from time to time as a little boy. But then they started to drift away from the church, and my grandmother Janet Montgomery, her husband, Albert, and my aunt Alexandra (Alex) Mealy took over. They were very religious and made me go to their church, the Myrtle Street Methodist Church. Billy Hoffman was also a member, as was my cousin Peggy who now lives in Sanford, Florida. It turned out that the change was a very good thing for me. The youth fellowship at the church was an opportunity to socialize and offered an alternative to the shadier elements of the gang I was hanging out with.

My grandparent, Janet and Albert Montgomery.

On Sundays, we'd all go to the service together. My Aunt Alex sang in the choir, and I'd sit with my grandmother and grandfather and make faces at her to see if I could break her up.

Afterwards, we went to my aunt's house for Sunday dinner—usually meat loaf. Then we went upstairs to my grandmother's (they lived in the same house) and had something more to eat—often meat loaf again.

I remember once saying to my Aunt Alex, "Do you think our family will ever be able to afford something besides meat loaf?"

My parents and their friends didn't talk much about politics. I never knew if my dad was a Democrat or Republican. He never told us how he voted, not even in presidential elections. When a new mayor was elected in Scranton, he appointed Cubby Rozelle, Ken's father, as superintendant of schools—that's the extent to which politics entered our lives.

Instead, my parents liked to talk about fishing, hunting, my dad's work, my mom's job at the hospital and all the different doctors in the neighborhood, as well as what was going on with the families of their friends.

They did smoke cigarettes, a habit I'm glad I never picked up. They both liked Raleighs, and each went through at least two packs a day. My mom saved the coupons on the back. She collected them in packets with rubber bands wrapped around and stockpiled them until she had enough to pick something from the Raleigh gift magazine. One time she got us a toaster, another time, a picnic basket.

Most of my memories from high school revolve around sports. I played varsity football for Scranton Tech during my junior and senior years. Our team was the Red Raiders. Billy Hoffman was the quarterback, I played fullback and halfback. We'd play both ways for 60 minutes, so I was a defensive back, too.

In the spring, I played baseball—mostly in the outfield—and was the shot putter on the track team. On weekends, we'd play sandlot baseball and softball at the Petersburg Silk Mill. We were always there for one reason or another.

As star athletes, we ranked high on the high school social ladder and did a lot of dating. After football games, we'd go to Chick's Diner on Moosic Street, which descends the hill from Nay Aug Park parallel to the Roaring Brook, down toward the bridge that crosses the river into downtown where Scranton University has a lot of property. Chick's was an old-fashioned, stainless steel diner owned by a Greek family that offered good home cooking and is still there today.

Another favorite hangout was Texas Wiener, off Lackawanna Avenue. The owner, whose name was Mr. Karampolis, would line up the hot-dog buns on his bare arms, put the wieners on, splash hot sauce over them, garnish them with mustard and onions, and slam them shut. He had scars all over his arms.

Joe Pacifico, who everyone called "Razz," was one of the first guys to have a car—he'd borrow his dad's Buick and we'd go to a drive-in movie theater or Chick's Diner. He lived in a beautiful house on Richter Avenue along the Roaring Brook. I spent a lot of time there. We'd gather at his house in the evening and head out to carouse, meeting up with girls and going to one of the night spots.

There were a couple of places where we could go dancing, even as kids in high school—bars with dance floors and live bands. We couldn't drink, but we could dance. A lot of my friends were great jitterbugs. Like Joe Pacifico, who wasn't much of an athlete, but made up for it by being tall, dark-haired and handsome, and nimble on his feet. I wasn't much of a dancer, but I could hold my own, and I excelled at slow dancing.

Billy and I did a lot of double-dating in high school—we even dated some of the same girls—but it was never anything serious.

We drank beer on the sly and once in while even had some cocktails. My parents always had beer in the house—Stegmeier, Gibbons and Ballentine—and no one minded me having an occasional brewski.

From left to right: Joe Pacifico, Pat Trunzo, Billy Hoffman, Joe Pacifico's cousin and Steve Wojdak.

Just before the start of my senior year, one of the more momentous and memorable events of my youth occurred.

July of 1955 was one of the driest months in Scranton's history. But late August made up for it in the form of Hurricane Diana, which sent storms raging across the whole Lackawanna River Valley. As a result, the Roaring Brook swelled and started to overflow its embankment. Joe Pacifico's house was located in the flood zone, and occasionally during the spring when the snows melted, there was some water in the basement, but nothing serious had ever happened. This time it was different.

On the evening of August 18, we were ready to go to Joe's house, but when we came to the Ash Street Bridge, the water was so high that we couldn't walk across. We stayed the night at Mr. Bucky's house, which was higher up on the hill on safe ground. To get there, we used a rope that Mr. Bucky threw to us. Billy Hoffman tied it around his waist. Because he was a good swimmer, he figured he could make it across where the current wasn't too strong yet. When he did, he threw the rope back over to us, and Joe and I followed him.

As the waters kept rising, the Roaring Brook more than lived up to its name, tearing down the hill with a vengeance, carrying all kinds of dangerous debris in its rushing waters. When the community center just north of Ash Street disintegrated with a big crashing sound, the remains swept downstream and destroyed most of Richter Avenue and Union Avenue, taking greenhouses, apartment buildings, Fachetti's Tavern and residential houses with them. We heard the crashing sound when Joe's house went.

By the next morning when the waters had receded and we finally were able to cross the bridge, all that was left of his home was the concrete front stoop. Fortunately, the family had been evacuated—Joe's mom and dad and his younger brother, Michael.

The Highfields, who lived right across the street from Joe, were not so lucky. Ellen and her husband, Elliott, had refused to leave at first. As the water kept rising, they realized that they were in serious trouble and climbed on the roof of their front porch. When the wall of water and debris came crashing down, it carried Ellen away, along with most of the house. Somehow Elliott managed to cling to a tree and miraculously survived.

The following morning, we came upon him sitting in the ford of a branch, and climbed up and helped him down to safety. It turned out that his wife had not been so lucky. Her body was recovered several miles down the river a day or so later on a porch railing.

The Petersburg section was hardest hit, but the Flats in South Scranton also sustained considerable damage. Mayor James T. Hanlon declared a state of emergency, which shut down the city for several days. The National Guard came with boats and a helicopter from Olmsted Air Force Base to rescue stranded homeowners.

A boat carries and old woman and two men to safety in the South Washington area on the night of August 18.

We worked tirelessly to help in any way we could, but it took weeks to clean up the all the debris in the disaster area. There were lots of houses whose basements were filled with mud, dead animals and other wreckage.

On a humorous side note, a day later, there was a picture in *The Scranton Times* that showed a soldier, from the rear, lending a hand to one of the survivors. He was wearing a military raincoat, and the caption identified him as a recently returned veteran from Korea. Well, that was actually me wearing the Marine coat my brother Bill had given me.

Helicopter rescue in South Scranton.

All in all, the flooding destroyed more than 50 homes and several bridges in Scranton and countless more throughout the Lackawanna River Valley. Fortunately, only two Scranton residents lost their lives, but more than 100 people were killed by the floods throughout the region. Many of the people who lost their homes did not come back and rebuild. Their insurance policies covered fire but not flood damage, so they were left high and dry in every sense of the words. Some of them moved outside the city away from the rivers to higher, safer ground. Others picked up what remained of their belongings and left the state for good.

Slowly the city recovered, and we were able to return to our normal routines.

Me catching a touchdown pass from Billy Hoffman in the 1955 Thanksgiving football game.

On Thanksgiving Day of 1955, we finished our high school football career in fine style, with me catching a touchdown pass from Billy Hoffman. It was the high point of the game for us, because we ended up losing to Central High and my friend Steve Wojdak, who was quarterbacking that team.

We did play one more time on the "dream team" in the county and city all-star game, in which the best players from Scranton competed against each other. Billy, Steve and I were picked for the city team. In those days, the game was played in the winter right after Thanksgiving, and the ground was solid ice, harder than a concrete floor, colder and a lot more slippery. It was impossible to get any footing, and the game ended in a nothing-nothing tie. Nowadays, the organizers are smarter and hold the all-star game in the spring on grass.

As we headed into our last semester, many of my friends were starting to make plans for their future. My friend Billy was going to go to Indiana University of Pennsylvania. Steve Wojdak was headed for higher education, too. Some kids I knew were going to join their father's or uncle's businesses, others planned to go into the military. I figured I wasn't going to college—I didn't have the grades, money or inclination. For a while, I wanted to be a state trooper like my dad. I even went to visit the barracks in Berwick where he had worked, to have a look and make up my mind.

But then I was approached by Don Grahamer and Frank Klassner, two young men from our neighborhood who were in the drilling business. Don, who was my brother Bill's age, had grown up near Joe Pacifico and had attended Scranton Tech, too. He'd been working as a driller for a couple of years after a stint in the Army. Frank was seven or eight years my senior. A lot of guys from the neighborhood went into that business, including Tom Ritchie (who was a foreman) and his son Bobby, Happy Jackson, and Kenny Davis—everyone called him Buddy.

Frank and Don knew my family—blue collar with good values—and knew I was a hard-working kid. They came to my house a few weeks before graduation, explained what drilling for soil and core samples was all about, and asked me if I wanted to join up and become a helper. It sounded like good work and good money, and I didn't hesitate long before saying yes.

As high school came to an end, I took one of the cheerleaders, Diane Betti, to the prom. I still see her occasionally in Florida, since she and her husband, Nick, have a townhouse on Longboat Key and play a lot of golf there.

One of the girls I graduated with was Betty Gillette, the cousin of my brother Bill's first wife, Shirley. She was in the band and the school orchestra and on the student council, and she is now the minister at Myrtle Street Methodist Church. We recently met at our 50th reunion and reminisced about old times. Sometimes it feels like a small world.

On the "Senior Inventory" page near the beginning of my yearbook, I am listed first as "Mr. Athlete." The paragraph next to my class picture features my nickname, "Crick," my grade school— William Prescott, and the area of study I focused on: Practical Arts, which meant industrial classes. Then there is a list of my activities— football, baseball, lettermen's club, track, newspaper and yearbook, followed by a two-line rhyme:

> A helping hand ready to lend,
> Always there when you need a friend.

I'm glad to say that it was true then, and it has been one of the important mottos in my life.

Some of my friends took off time before college. I didn't get much of a summer break, however. In fact, three days after graduation on May 19, 1956, I left for New Jersey and my first job as a driller.

Chapter 3
FIRST SOUNDINGS

I went to work for Giles Drilling Company and was teamed as a helper with Buddy Davis. I don't remember much about that first job, except that it was taking test borings and core samples in the swamps of the New Jersey meadows.

Drilling for core samples is a physically demanding job.

There are basically two parts to it: Driving casing and drilling for soil and core samples.

You take a drill rig to the future site of a large building, bridge or other structure that requires solid foundations, and you penetrate down through the top soil—what we call the overburden—until you hit hard rock. Depending on the requirements of the structure to be built, you may get several soil samples along the way and then drill into the rock to a certain depth to retrieve core samples. The samples then get analyzed in a lab, and from the results the engineers can tell how many pounds per square foot the ground will bear and how far down they will need to excavate to lay the foundations. The core samples may come from a depth of 5 feet or 300 feet. Sometimes you have to drill through layers of loose or soft rock, like shale or limestone, or even deeper into the rock itself until you get to harder, more solid strata, such as gneiss or basalt.

The crew for the job usually consists of the driller and his helper and a consulting engineer who tells them where to put the hole, when to take samples and how deep to go. The driller is in charge of the rig, the sampling and all the written logs pertaining to the job. The helper basically provides muscle.

To drive casing through the soil with a pipe 4 to 6 inches in diameter, you use a hammer, a 300-pound weight that gets dropped from 2½ feet up onto the pipe. The drill rig has a cylinder called a cathead which winds up rope with a diesel or compressor-driven motor. The rope runs up in the air over a shiv wheel and down the other side to the hammer—that's the bolen—and lifts it up into the air. There is a hole in the hammer, and when you release it, the weight slides down and hits the drive ring, so it doesn't crush the coupling end, pounding the pipe into the ground. BA-DA-BOOM, BADA-BOOM, BADA-BOOM—it makes an ear-splitting racket.

Casing comes in 5 to 10 foot lengths, and as you go down you keep adding pipe, connecting the threaded ends and screwing it as tight as you can with chain tongs, just like on an oil rig. It's hard work lifting the pipe in place and holding it with a clamp until it's attached and ready to be driven further down.

If you're going to take a soil sample, you switch to a 140-pound hammer and count the number of blows it takes to drive the casing one foot. Depending on the composition and density of the soil, it may take 6 blows or 500. The consultants tell you when and how many samples to take. Sometimes they may want it every foot and half, at other times, when you reach to a certain depth, they may want it every 5 feet.

It's called a split spoon sample. You use a two-foot-long pipe at the bottom of the rod that is lowered into the hole. The pipe, made from two hollow halves put together, has a threaded section at the bottom, called the nose, and a header that holds it together at the top and attaches it to the rod. After you pull the pipe out, you take it off the rod, remove the head and nose and crack it against something solid, splitting the two halves. You lay it on the ground and the consultant indicates which section to use as the soil sample. You put that in a glass jar and scratch on the lid at what depth the sample was collected and how many blows it took to get there.

When you hit the foundation rock strata, you try to seat the casing on the rock and drive it in some. Then you wash it out and put a diamond bit through the casing—it's a ring of diamond bits at the bottom of a smaller hollow pipe, called a core barrel. As that barrel rotates, it drills into the rock and pushes up a narrow cylinder of the strata inside the pipe—the core sample. On solid rock, you drill a 5-foot or 10-foot core barrel. When you've reached the right depth, you snap it off. A core spring snaps into place to hold the sample inside. Then you pull the core barrel out of the hole, break the bit off, take the core out and store it in a long, narrow, wooden core box. In the course of days and weeks on a particular job, you may take five or six core samples from different places, or maybe a hundred.

When you're done, you retrieve the casing from the ground. You put the hammer back on the drive head, only this time with a different coupling and bang on it upwards, reversing its impact and pulling the casing out of the hole—it's called bumping pipe. Then you load it on the truck. You hardly ever leave casing in the ground, unless it broke off.

You either have a rack truck where the drill rig is mounted on the back, or a stationary rig on the ground on skids or wheels. The latter gets put on the truck via ramps. Then you head to the next job or back to the yard to refit your rig. Because every job is different, you might need a different drill rig, different-sized pipe or different-sized core barrels.

It's hard, physical work—surrounded all day long by the noise of the hammer blows, the whirring drill, and the motor or compressor running, and the smells of diesel fuel and pipe dope on the threads. It's a dangerous job, too. I know a lot of guys who've had fingers busted or broken off. Donnie Grahamer and I were lucky. We still have all our fingers.

One guy we knew, Frank Gregory, who worked for the Warren George Drilling Company, was not so lucky. Frank was 5'10", weighed about 180 pounds, and was strong as a bull. We actually saw him pick up a 300-pound hammer by the ear handles and put it on a pickup truck. He was something of a wild man when we got to know him, but later on he became the owner of that company and remained very active, going out on the jobs to keep the men busy and show them how to do the work.

Frank was with a drill rig on a barge in the Hudson River just south of the George Washington Bridge, taking samples on the bottom of the river. It was raining, which makes conditions treacherous. When the rope gets wet, it has a tendency to cross itself as it wraps around the cathead, and it can stall out the motor.

Apparently, Frank was showing his men how to bump pipe when his arm got caught in the rope by the cathead, and it sucked him 30 feet up into the air, into the shiv wheel and cut his arm off.

Fortunately, Frank survived the accident, and he continued as the owner of his drilling company until he retired a few years back.

Nowadays, you have to take all kinds of safety precautions. The men are required to wear earphones, steel-toed shoes and hard hats. They can't have any cuffs on their shirts, so that they don't get caught in a chain or rope. But in my days, we didn't have any of that. We had a driller's union—affiliated with Carpenters and Joiners of America—and I signed up when I graduated to become a driller.

As a result, there were some rules and restrictions about when we could and couldn't drill. In rain, heat or cold, there was a point when you had to stop working. The consultants would make the decision. They might say, "Okay, we can't work in these conditions." Then we'd wait a couple of hours to see if things changed. It was called stand-by time.

You showed up on the job. That didn't mean you had to go to work that day. You might end up sitting in your car or truck. If it rained too hard, you got paid a couple of hours and went home. That was called show-up time. It's the way the union works.

But for the most part, we were out there all the time, year-around—summer, winter, it made no difference. If the frost went down three or four feet, it meant nothing to us. We could drill through that in minutes. In fact, we often preferred the winter months, even if it sometimes meant frost-bitten fingers. It's far easier to work in mud or a swamp when they're frozen than to try crossing soft muck and mire with a rig on wheels or a skid.

In any case, I don't remember any details about my first job in New Jersey, probably because the second was so exciting. After a month or so, Frank Klassner asked me to join him and Donnie Grahamer on a job for a Texas Tower off the coast of Martha's Vineyard in Massachusetts. He would be the driller, and Donnie and I, his helpers.

In the 1950s, the U.S. Air Force had the idea of putting up a series of five radar towers 100 miles or so off the coast of Maine, Massachusetts and New York to extend our defense warning system against Russian naval vessels. They were called Texas Towers because, standing on three legs in the middle of the ocean, they looked like the oil rigs in the Gulf of Mexico. The original plans called for five towers, but the Air Force ended up building only three. The first one was up already, and we were hired to do the test borings in the sands of the ocean floor for the second one—it was actually called TT3—off the Nantucket Shoals.

The Texas Tower with the platform floating on the water.

When we drove up to Fall River, Massachusetts, we expected to head out to sea right away, but we ended up staying in a hotel there for a week because the fog was too thick to navigate off-shore.

When the fog finally lifted, they picked us and our equipment up on a sea-going tug that had been modified for construction purposes and took us to our destination 120 miles out, right past where the wrecks of the *Stockholm* and *Andrea Doria* were lying. They were just floating the large triangular platform of the tower into place. It was still bobbing on the surface of the water, and we were transferred first to a barge and from there onto the deck of the tower.

For the next week, we lounged around in the crew quarters, reading and playing cards, getting paid 24 hours a day for another seven days, while the platform was being raised hydraulically.

*The underside of the platform being raised.
Note the barge on the water to the lower left.*

There were 11 legs sunk into the ocean, three of them permanent. The other eight were just tacked on for support during construction. The three permanent support legs were 20 feet in diameter, and the platform was 210 feet on each side and 20 feet tall. When it was finally in place 100 feet up in the air, they built us a little square platform jutting out over the water off one of the sides. It was welded on and hanging about 10 feet over the edge.

Our drilling rig platform, extending beyond the edge of the tower.

And that's where we put our drilling machine and worked, protected only by a flimsy-looking guardrail. We put casing down 100 feet through the air and through 80 feet of water before we reached the ocean bottom. From there we drilled another 100 feet down into the sand of the seabed to make sure there was solid foundation under the three legs. The way the towers were designed, the building crew would excavate the sand from the hollow legs and dump it in the ocean, and then the weight of the tower would push the legs further down into the sand until the whole structure became locked in place, stationary and stable in the ocean.

It was tough work. There was always a strong, salty breeze. One time it blew off Frank Klassner's hard hat and we watched it sail straight down. By the time it hit the ocean it was so small we could hardly make it out.

The reason the job required two helpers was that we had to hold the drill rod in midair with a sliding iron as we attached them to one another and lowered them into the casing. The sliding iron had a hole which the rods slid through and a long handle. When you put downward pressure on the handle, the angle would hold the rod in place and prevent it from sliding. Frank would hold the iron while Donnie and I attached the next section and tightened the flush joint. Then he would let up and guide the rod until it hit bottom and we'd resume drilling.

Frank Klassner, foreman and driller.

The rods were 10-foot lengths, and by the time we were drilling deep into the sand, we'd be going down the length of more than two football fields, which meant holding up 20 to 30 rods. We'd bet Frank Klassner that he couldn't do it. Then we'd sneak a slightly thinner rod in on top (rods get worn down from frequent use) and WHOOP—it would slip. Sometimes Frank managed to hold it, sometimes he didn't and it would slide into the casing pipe before he could catch it. Of course it didn't go down much farther than half a rod's length, and we would "fish" for the top and screw on the next rod enough to bring it up and tighten up the joint.

Frank Klassner and Donnie Grahamer.

It took us two weeks to drill down 100 feet into the seabed. We never hit rock, but by the time we reached that depth the sand was so tightly packed that, for all practical purposes, we might just as well have. The Air Force engineers were satisfied. And then we had to retrieve all of our core barrel and casing pipes, 10 feet at a time.

The way we got off the tower was to ride in a circular basket that looked like a basket on top of a rubber tire with a lift line attached—everyone called it the donut. I'm not afraid of heights, but one trip down to the barge, dangling in the air high above the water, was enough for me. And after we made it to the harbor in Fall River, I was glad to be on solid ground again.

Our job was over, but the saga of the Texas Towers was not. The Air Force built one more, two short of the projected five. The last one was located in even deeper waters, which created structural problems for the legs,

Above: The donut.
Below: Frank and Donnie in the donut, looking over their shoulders.

so the legs had to be reinforced with special struts to make them more stable.

But the Towers never quite worked as predicted. They rocked in the fierce N'easters that roared through the area in the winters. Waves and ocean currents undermined the legs at sea bottom. When Hurricane Donna came through in late 1960, it damaged the third tower, which had been built about four miles southeast of New York City. And in early January 1961, disaster struck. A fierce winter storm destroyed it completely. All 27 crew members were lost, many of them I had met when we'd worked on the one off the Nantucket Shoals. After that, the Air Force abandoned the remaining two towers—the development of ICBM missiles made them less useful anyway—and by 1963 they had been decommissioned and demolished.

For me, however, my time on the Texas Tower was one of the highlights of my career as a driller, an unforgettable experience. Plus, Frank, Donnie and I came home to Scranton flush with cash and good stories. With my earnings, I bought a '57 Chevy, a red two-door hardtop, whitewall tires and silver fins on the back fenders. It cost me about $3,000 cash, and I became quite the man about town.

Chapter 4
WORK AND PLAY

After the Texas Towers, I went from job to job, wherever Giles Drilling sent us—Washington, Maryland, Massachusetts, New York, Connecticut. We did test borings for building, bridges and highways in the swamps of East New Jersey and in the Bowery in New York City. Much of the time, we didn't know what we were drilling for. We just followed the directions from the consulting engineers and put our holes down wherever they told us to, and we didn't ask what it was all about.

One of the more interesting jobs was taking test borings for a new section of the Norfolk Portsmouth Bridge Tunnel in Virginia. Our drill rig was on a barge smack in middle of the Elizabeth River. We were drilling into the riverbed when a coast guard cutter came by, blowing its horn. The crew shouted at us through a bullhorn, "Get off the river!"

Well, when the coast guard tells you to move, you move. We pulled our drill up as fast as we could, hoisted our anchor and headed for shore, leaving the casing pipe sticking out of the water so we could find the spot again later. As we were taking off, we looked back and saw the battleship New Jersey coming down the river. As it cruised past, the wake from that monster vessel rocked our tiny barge as if we were in a hurricane.

I learned the trade quickly and after a year, at age 19, I am proud to say, I became the youngest driller in the Tri-State Area.

Me taking a break on a drilling job in Trenton, New Jersey.

We worked hard and played hard. When we were out of town on a job, we got an allotment for room and board, so we stayed in rooming houses—they were cheaper than motels—in order to stretch our per diems farther. We played a lot of cards with the other lodgers, usually penny-ante poker and pinochle. But most evenings, we'd have a quick shower and a change of clothes and get ready to hit the town. If we happened to be in a city with a major league baseball team and Paul Foytack happened to be playing for the Detroit Tigers, we'd go to see him pitch. But most of the time, we'd head out to a bar, have a few pops, play some pool, come back and lie down for a couple of hours, and be back up the next morning for another full day of work. I think we were familiar with every bar from Boston to Baltimore in the towns where we stayed. Along the way Donnie Grahamer and I became very good friends, and we've remained close in retirement. He and his son, Donnie Jr., are both members of our hunting camp in Pike County.

On weekends, we'd drive home to Scranton from wherever the company had sent us. I lived with my parents.

One day I came home with a monkey. His name was Chico, like the Marx Brother who wore a goofy hat and always played the piano, and he had a yellow tip on his tail. I'd seen him in a pet shop looking forlorn and bought him on a lark. My mom and dad just about killed me when I walked into the house with him, but they fell in love with Chico all the same. My dad even built a fancy wire cage for him in the basement.

Pretty soon, they were taking him along at night to Chick's Diner—you could get away with things like that in those days. I used to put him on a leash, and he'd walk on two legs holding on to it for balance. Whenever I took him to Globe, the big clothing store in downtown Scranton, the sales clerks would ooh and ah over him and ask me to bring him up to the other floors to entertain the shoppers. Strangers would stop to talk to me and ask questions about him. Lots of girls, too. Chico definitely was what they nowadays call a "chick magnet."

But he could also be nasty. He bit my fingers a couple of times. And he was a sneak-thief. When I drove in my Chevy, he'd sit on my left shoulder right by the window. Often when I pulled over, kids would come running up to look at him. One time, a little boy was carrying an ice cream cone. Chico reached out and grabbed it and, before anyone could blink, he'd bitten off the bottom and was sucking the ice cream. In the process, it ran down all over his hairy arms.

He also loved to chew gum. But his favorite treat was chocolate Tasty Cakes, which came wrapped in cellophane, three to a package. One time a kid came over with a pack and—boom-bam—quick as a wink, Chico had one in his foot, one in his hand and one in his mouth.

When I put him on the clothes line out in the backyard, he'd hold on with all four paws. No matter how much I shook the rope, I couldn't get him off. He'd hold on swinging upside down and every which way, loving every moment of it.

Chico was a lot of fun, but my job had me travel too much and I had to get rid of him, so I donated him to the Nay Aug Park Zoo. Whenever I got home on weekends, I'd go to visit him. As soon as I went through the gate, I'd yell, "Chico! Chico!" and he'd start screaming and making a racket. Before long, he had the lions and tigers in an uproar.

During the summer, Billy Hoffman came home from college and played baseball for a local semi-pro team, the Petersburg Blue Devils. My dad, who was very active in the neighborhood, worked with the team as a trainer. I went to see all his weekend games. Once in a while, when they were a man short, they asked me to stand in, and I did, mostly as an outfielder.

Come fall, I played for the Don Juan Wines, a football team sponsored by a local liquor distributor. I also played volleyball at the YMCA with Ken Rozelle. We developed good camaraderie, going out to eat and hefting a few beers afterwards.

In the evenings, I went out on dates and had a fine time until Sunday night when we drillers all piled into cars to head back to work. We were young, single and didn't have a care in the world. Life was good. And about to get even better.

Me in uniform for the Don Juan Wines football team.

Shortly after I started out in the drilling business, a young woman was hired as a medical secretary at Hahnemann Hospital in the records department where my mom was working. Her name was Barbara Sumski and she had just graduated from South Catholic High School. She was smart, spirited and attractive. My mom, who was quite the matchmaker, wanted us to get together. So she kept talking Barbara up to me while telling her that she really should make a point of meeting me.

For a while Barbara didn't seem all that interested, but my mom was nothing if not persistent, so she finally said, "Okay, I'll meet your son when he comes home this weekend. Give me a call and you can come over Saturday or Sunday afternoon."

So that Saturday, I put on a pair of khaki pants, a dress shirt and my suede leather dirty bucks. Then my mom and I jumped into my fancy '57 Chevy and drove to Cedar Avenue in South Scranton. Like me, Barbara was still living at home with her parents. It was customary for young people, especially girls, to do that, at least until they got married. They had a good, familiar, protected place to stay, and because they were earning money, they could contribute to the rent, which helped their parents out.

When we got to her house, Barbara was sitting on the porch. She came to the curb to greet us. It was the first time I saw her, and I remember it like it was yesterday. She was dressed in plaid slacks and a blouse that accentuated her beautiful figure. When she laughed, her blond hair shook and her eyes sparkled. I was immediately taken by her. And impressed. Sometimes when people talk up a person, they paint them in such glowing colors that when you finally meet them, you can't help but be disappointed. But in Barbara's case, my mom had not exaggerated. She was beautiful and full of life, and she had a great smile.

After checking out my car, she took us inside and introduced us to her parents. Her father, Bart (Bartholomew) was a big, tall man, and her mother, Albina, was such a gorgeous woman, I could see right away where Barbara had gotten her beauty. We all sat down and had sodas in the living room. It felt a bit awkward, our parents there and looking us over—this was almost like an old-fashioned courting visit—but Barbara and I survived it well enough, and we decided to get together later that day. I took her to a baseball game at the Petersburg Silk Mill field to watch Billy Hoffman play. It turned out that Barbara loved sports, although she was not especially athletic herself, and she liked all of my friends—Billy, Steve, Joe Pacifico and Ken Rozelle. After I'd taken her home, I met up with them later that night and I told them all, "I'm going to marry that girl."

For the next two years, Barbara and I spent just about every weekend together. She would come and watch me play football and volleyball. Or we would spend the afternoon at Lake Wallenpaupack with the whole gang picknicing, swimming and waterskiing. At times we'd double-date with Billy Hoffman or Steve Wojdak and their latest girlfriends, have a bite to eat at one of the local hangouts, see a movie at a drive-in, or go dancing at one of the bars.

Barbara and me out on a date.

As Barbara and I got closer, we talked about getting married and starting a family. I liked her parents and they liked me, but they were devout Catholics, so I had to convert. For six weeks, I went to class with a young priest to learn all of the Catholic teachings. Father Timlan couldn't have been more than 25 years old, and I thought he looked like Christ, he was so handsome. His hands were soft and alabaster white. He later became the bishop of Scranton and is now retired.

When I finished the course and went through the conversion ceremony to become a Catholic, Father Timlan gave Barb and me a cross as a wedding present. It hangs in my bedroom to this day.

Our different religious backgrounds created an additional snag. I had always wanted Billy Hoffman to act as my best man, but he was a Methodist, so he couldn't perform that role at a Catholic ceremony. I had to tell him that Steve Wojdak would be taking his place. He understood and attended the wedding with his girlfriend, who also happened to be one of the bridesmaids.

Barbara and me at our wedding.

Barbara and I got married in Saint Mary's Church in South Scranton on May 24, 1958. Everyone we knew came to the wedding—all our friends and families, including my parents, my brother Butch, my aunts and uncles, Barbara's two sisters, Lorraine and Dolores, and her older brother, Joe, who was the manager for US Airways at the Scranton-Wilkes Barre Airport. I wish my brother Bill could have been there, too, but he was stationed aboard an aircraft carrier at the time and couldn't get a furlough.

Billy Hoffman, me and Steve Wojdak at my wedding.

It was a festive wedding, although we didn't have much of a honeymoon because I had to go back to work on Monday. We moved into my parent's house, and not much changed in our routine. I'd be gone during the week, and Barb would work with my mom at the hospital. On weekends, I'd be home. We'd go out together with our friends and she'd come to my ball games.

In the summer of 1959, I had one of my more interesting drilling jobs, doing test borings for the anchorage of the Verrazano

Narrows Bridge that was being built to connect Brooklyn and Staten Island. Named after the Italian explorer Giovanni Verrazano, the first European navigator to enter the New York Harbor and the Hudson River, it would become the largest suspension bridge in the United States. It's now best known as the starting point of the annual New York City Marathon, and it's quite a spectacular sight when tens of thousands of runners descend the bridge on the Brooklyn side.

One of the pleasures of that job was that I had my dad working with me as my helper. We drilled on both the Brooklyn and Staten Island sides, taking soil samples and, once we got into the rock, core samples to make sure the concrete foundations could support the anchorage cable works, which would take the tremendous weight and strain of holding up the bridge.

It was a huge construction site and by the time we were called in, excavations had already begun. Altogether, it took more than 10,000 men before the bridge was completed. The upper deck opened on June 28, 1964, and the lower deck took five more years to finish. By then, we were long gone, of course, but I got a medallion for being a worker on the bridge, which I recently gave to my son, Bobby, to put on the end of a chain for a pocket watch.

A couple of months later, Donnie Grahamer and I were sent to Lake Placid in upstate New York, the future site of the 1980 Winter Olympics, to drill for missile silos for the U.S. Army. It was a popular winter sport resort already, and Arthur Godfrey used to come up and do his TV shows from there, although we never ran into him. We made Lake Placid our base and headed out to drill all over the area, including the small communities of Tupper Lake and Saranac Lake. We were cross shifting with another crew—a friend from Scranton named Freddy Hawkins and his brother as helper—working 12-hour shifts each to keep the drill rig going around the clock and get the work done more quickly. We switched day and night shifts with the other team at the end of each week.

It was bitterly cold at night and early in the mornings. We were drilling at the bottom of Whiteface Mountain, at 4,867 feet the fifth highest peak in New York state. There wasn't much of an overburden and a lot of places had rocky outcrops—half-exposed boulders and stones sticking out of the ground. Drilling was tough because we we'd hit granatic gneiss, one of the hardest rocks on earth. It was tearing up the diamond bits and we were going at a snail's pace. We kept sending the bits out for analysis to determine what type we needed to do the job more efficiently, but the lab could never figure it out.

As a result, when we finally got a hole deep enough in the ground, the engineers would come and conduct a seismic test, using dynamite. We were responsible for setting the charges. We carried the dynamite in the trunk of our car and the blasting caps in the glove compartment. We'd tape the dynamite to a long stick —the engineers would tell us how much was needed—and lower into the hole with a wire. Everyone would stand back when we were ready to blow the hole. We'd touch the wires to a battery in the car or to the Magneto (the generator motor on the drill rig) and KABOOM. The explosion would blow the wire and sand and gravel 20 to 30 feet in the air. Often the wire would get wound around the shiv wheel and the derrick, and we'd have to climb up to get it untangled.

The engineers would record the explosion with a seismograph to determine how hard the rock was. These instruments, which are used to measure earthquakes, were so sensitive that they would register a cow walking in a field nearby.

The farmers were curious and asked what we were doing, but we were sworn to secrecy by the military and gave them some fictitious story. The local communities didn't find out until much later that they were going to be repositories for missiles. One day the local newspaper sent a reporter and photographer to our site, and the next day there was a picture of Donnie and me and a headline that asked humorously, "What Are These Fellers Drillin' Fer?"

One weekend our wives, Barbara and Helen Grahamer came for a visit. Barbara was already pregnant with our daughter, Michelle. We went out to a restaurant and did some sightseeing. There were iceskaters on the lakes and daredevils flying off the big ski jump. We had a good time together, and I'm fairly certain that it was that weekend that Donnie's wife got pregnant with their first child.

Sometime after we finished that job, the army built the silos and put missiles into them. Last year, when I went to see my grandson Travis, who goes to Paul Smith's College, an environmental school near Lake Placid, we drove to the top of Whiteface Mountain. From the treeless summit we could see hundreds of square miles of forest, lakes and mountains stretching from Canada to Vermont. An old park ranger greeted us, and I told him that the last time I'd been there had been nearly 50 years earlier when I was drilling for missile sites. He said, "I remember those missiles coming through town. We all watched the army convoys that brought them."

Since then, the missiles have been decommissioned, and the silos are now used for storage.

Our daughter, Michelle, who is called Shelly by everyone, was born on December 28, 1959. At 7 months, she was a premie and had to be delivered by Caesarian birth. She spent a week or so at the hospital, and by the time we brought her home from the hospital, we had completed our moving in with Barbara's parents. Their house was bigger than the one my folks lived in and had an extra room we could use as a nursery. Albina and Bart were wonderful people, and they loved me as if I were their own son.

Bart was a welder and a part-time police captain in Moosic, the Greenwood section of South Scranton. Many a Friday night when I came home for the weekend, I'd ride in the police cruiser with him for a couple of hours. We never saw any action, but he was good to talk to, and the poker games we had in his neighborhood bar afterward were a lot of fun. He nicknamed me Maverick, after the popular TV show running on ABC which featured James Garner and Jack Kelly as Bret and Bart Maverick, traveling poker-players in the Wild West.

Bart and Albina Sumski.

Like my mom, Albina was a great cook. The house often smelled of cabbage and kielbasa, which she made from scratch.

She also made pigs in the blanket, which we called galumphies, as well as pierogi, special potato dumplings. I can still remember her sitting on the back porch, grating the horseradish from her garden, tears streaming down her face.

Albina had worked in one of the Scranton silk mills and got cirrhosis of the liver, probably from inhaling carbon tetra chloride, which was used as a cleaning fluid, as she was packing up the boxes. She got deathly ill and sued the company. By the time I knew her, she couldn't work anymore, so she helped out with the baby.

One night, shortly after we'd brought Shelly home, we heard a commotion in her crib—she was choking. My mother-in-law heard her, too. She rushed to the nursery and picked her up. Shelly had something in her throat and was already turning blue. Albina didn't hesitate. She gave Shelly mouth-to-mouth resuscitation and sucked out whatever was obstructing her until she started breathing again. There is no doubt in my mind that Albina and her quick thinking saved Shelly's life.

After that our lives continued on a smooth trajectory. I continued to work from early Monday morning until Friday evening. On weekends, Barbara would come and watch me play football and volleyball, bringing Shelly along in the stroller. Every Sunday morning we'd go to the Minooka Bakery for prune and cheese Danish and homemade bread.

At that time, Pete Carlisimo Sr., whose son became a well-known college basketball coach for Seton Hall and later on in the NBA as well, was the football coach for Scranton University. He heard about me playing on the Don Juan Wines and offered me a full scholarship to play for him, and on the volleyball team as well. Unfortunately, I didn't have a high enough score on the college entrance examination, so he encouraged me to go to night school.

I tried it for several months, but it didn't work out. I was married, had a baby, and I was never much of a scholar. Besides, I was making good money. With all my activities and limited time, I had to decline—college just wasn't in the cards for me.

On January 11, 1962, my son, Bobby, was born. When I first saw him in the hospital's nursery, lying in the crib, I called him "My Superman," and I continue to call him that today.

I remember going out to a lot of drive-in movie theaters with Barbara and the kids. We'd put their pajamas on ahead of time, get some popcorn or hot dogs, and watch the picture together. Invariably, both kids would be asleep in the backseat before the movie was over, and we'd have to carry them upstairs to bed when we got home.

By then, Barbara and I were renting an apartment on Moosic Street. We needed more room, and with our growing family, it was time to be on our own. The place was on the third floor of an apartment building right along the route of the ill-fated truck that went out of control, carrying a load of bananas a few years later. The long hill coming down off Lake Scranton is so steep that there is a warning sign at the top for trucks to shift into low gear. The young driver must have fallen asleep behind the wheel, or his brakes failed—whatever the case, he lost control of his 35-foot semi trailer rig and it tore down Moosic Street at 90 miles an hour, taking out mail boxes and fences and side-swiping several cars. At the bottom of the hill, where the road takes a sharp turn onto the bridge into downtown Scranton, it crashed, killing the driver and spilling bananas all over the place. Harry Chapin, the folk singer, wrote a song about it, called "30,000 Pounds of Bananas," and recorded it on his 1974 album "Verities & Balderdash."

Barb and I were a happy young couple, but I was getting tired of the commute to Giles Drilling in New Jersey, and I hated being away from home all week long. It was hard on Donnie and Helen Grahamer and their three young children(Gail, Don Jr. and Holly), too. We all kept talking about it for some time and finally made the decision in 1963 to leave Scranton and move closer to where our work was.

So one weekend, Donnie and I packed up our belongings and said good-bye. We used the same moving van on the same day to go to New Jersey. Our mover's name was Earl Beppler. I had worked for him in high school a couple of times when he needed extra help on a big job, and now he was helping us.

Bobby was still a baby and Shelly was 4 years old, and they went with Barb in our car. I had scouted out a place to rent in Scotch Plains, and Donnie took his family to Red Bank, New Jersey. We managed to do it all in one day and by Monday morning, we were back at work, but now we were able to come home at night.

Chapter 5
MOVING ON

It wasn't easy to leave Scranton behind and start a new life in a strange place, but while we were sad to go and missed our family, friends and community, we knew it was the best thing to do. And we were right. The commute from the Giles Drilling yard was only 20 miles, and it was great to be home every night after work. Most of the drilling work was in New York, Connecticut and right there in New Jersey—we spent months taking test borings for all the overpasses on Interstate 287 from Perth Amboy all the way to Bridgewater. Once in a while, there were still jobs that took us out of town for the whole week, but they were fewer and far in between.

We lived in a brand-new apartment on East Second Street and stayed there for a year. It was called Banner Homes, and we liked the neighborhood. Although it was suburban, it was just as friendly as Bunker Hill in Scranton. One day, Shelly went missing and we frantically searched the whole area for several hours. A number of our neighbors helped, too. Finally we got a call from the police station: "We have her, and she's sitting here eating an ice cream cone." I can't describe the relief we felt when we picked her up. She had just wandered off.

The owners and builders of Banner Homes were three Italian developers, and I got to know them quite well. When they started to develop a large tract in Hillsborough about 15 miles north of Princeton, putting up 30 or so homes there, they said to me, "Why do you pay us rent? Why don't you let us build you a house?"

Barb and I went to look at the development in the middle of farmland and corn fields one afternoon and liked what we saw. After we studied our finances and figured out we could afford it, we told the brothers to go ahead. I put in my own water well and did all the painting and landscaping myself, saving us a considerable amount of money. We ended up living there for most of the 1960s.

When Bobby and Shelly were young, Barb was a homemaker while I went to work. She cut the grass and took care of the kids and the garden. When they were both old enough to go to school, she went back to work as a secretary for the Gavazzi Tire Company in Bridgewater, a couple of miles away. During the summers, her sister Lorraine would come down from Scranton and babysit both of our children during her break from teaching high school.

Barbara and Billy Hoffman's wife, Mickey, kept in touch—he'd gotten married a few years after me and they had two boys. That was how we managed to stay close even when our lives went separate ways and Billy worked for Coca Cola. He'd met Mickey, who was an army brat, after he'd joined ROTC, became a lieutenant and then a helicopter pilot in the reserves. Later on, when their two boys would get into a fight, Mickey would dive right in and break it up, so they called her "Hurricane," and the nickname stuck. In those days, Billy lived in Buffalo, and part of his job was to periodically fly over Attica Prison—that was before the notorious riots in 1971—to keep the prisoners on their toes. They thought they were being spied on and never knew when his chopper would come by.

One weekend when I was working in the yard in Hillsborough, I heard a whap-whap sound in the distance. I looked down the road and saw a bubble helicopter coming into the town. As it came closer it kept flying lower and lower. The woman who lived two houses down from us was trying to wave it off with a towel, but it kept coming closer until it set down in my front yard. Out jumped Billy with a big grin on his face and he invited me to come for a ride. As I climbed into the chopper and Billy put the earphones on me, my son, Bobby, who was about 5 at the time and standing with a bunch of kids who had gathered quickly, started to cry when they yelled, "Oh, Mr. Kreilick is going to war!" I had to reassure him that I was coming back soon.

Then I took off in the chopper with Billy and got a bird's-eye tour of the area. We landed at a nearby airport where Billy had his car, and he drove me home. He'd done it just for a lark.

After he retired from the reserves as a colonel, Billy joined the corporate world and ended up as a senior vice president for Coca Cola with a high profile career. One time he was on the cover of *Fortune Magazine* for going to Europe to head up Coca Cola's operations in France. Among other successful business ventures, he bought up bottling companies and introduced vending machines to Paris.

My career as a driller could never match that prominence, although I did work on some important, if not glamorous, projects. One of the most interesting was taking the first soil and core samples for the World Trade Center in New York City. I was working for Haller Testing Laboratory out of Plainfield, New Jersey, on that job, and my dad was once again my helper.

The original location was to be in lower Manhattan near the Fulton Fish Market, but we actually took the first test boring up on Wall Street. As we put the first hole down, we hit solid rock at about 35 feet, which was good news. The consulting engineers made me drill five feet into the rock and take a core. We came out with nice sample of granitic gneiss, perfect for the massive towers of the World Trade Center. If you got a nice core, that was the end of the hole.

As other drillers showed up, Haller Lab sent a foreman, and we moved my rig right to a corner of the Fulton Fish Market. By the time we got there in the morning, the fish mongers were already busy at work, cleaning the fish that had come in from the boats—cutting off the heads, gutting and filleting them. The smell of fish was powerful and overwhelming, and by the time we'd spent our shift there, it was part of our clothes.

I put the hole down where the rock starts to drop off toward the East River. We'd take a spoon sample every five feet, counting the 140-pound hammer blows along the way. As we drove the casing down about 40 to 50 feet, we hit a layer of talc. Now, talc is one of the softest minerals in the world—in loose form it's known as talcum powder—so the consultant had me continue the hole. It was hard enough to drill into, but when we pulled the core barrel out, it would cave in so that we couldn't advance the casing. Normally a hole stays open, maintaining its integrity. You pull the core barrel out, take the diamond bit off, knock the core out, and store it in a box. Then you put the bit back on, tighten it up, drop the core barrel in, and—kerplumb—it drops right to the bottom, and you start drilling again.

But in this case, when we pulled the core barrel out and put the drill back in, it would hit right where we'd started before. We tried it several times, but each time the talc would collapse on the bottom of the hole.

We had to come up with something, so I had the idea of cementing the hole. When we pulled the core barrel out, we put a tremie pipe down as fast as we could—they're used to seal water wells—and poured cement in. As you pump the cement through the hole and pull the pipe out, the cement fills in the bottom. After we went home, the cement would harden overnight, and in the morning we could drill through it, put our core barrel in and go deeper. Then we'd have to repeat the process. Most of the time, the talc was so soft that it would crumble and wash out in the drilling water, and we never got much of a core sample even when we used a double-tube core barrel—which has a tube inside the drill barrel that doesn't spin.

By now, we were using 10-foot core barrels instead of the usual 5-foot to speed up the job. We kept going down, cementing and drilling, until we got to 320 feet and we still didn't hit rock bottom. At that point the engineers gave up and told us to abandon the hole. They had hoped we'd run through the talc bubble and be able to take a nice core, which would allow them to design a foundation that would hold the building. Another rig at the opposite corner of the Fulton Fish Market had hit hard rock at a shallow depth.

As a result of my findings they decided to move the World Trade Center 10 blocks uptown. Haller Lab didn't get the job for that location, so I moved on and never did the test borings for the actual towers. I have gone back to that exact corner of the Fulton Fish Market—after they remodeled it and turned into a shopping center—for old time's sake.

I was more than a month on that job, and ever since I've had a bad back. Everything had to be done by hand, putting the 10-foot rods in with a sliding iron and pulling them back out. It was back-breaking work—literally—and at some point, my lower vertebrae gave out from bending over and holding the weight up. My back started to hurt. By the time I got home at night, I could hardly get out of the car. I'd have to take a hot bath and then go to bed. The next morning, I'd have to lay on the floor to put my pants on, so I could go back to work.

I was only in my mid-20s, but something had gone in my L-5 vertebrae. Later it became arthritic, so when I've gone to doctors since, they tell me that there is nothing an operation can do for it. I wear a back plaster, which provides heat and support, when I play sports. The pain comes and goes, but I never lost a day's work over it, and it hasn't stopped me from any activities I wanted to do—play football or golf, or go horseback riding. I just can't lift anything heavy anymore.

Me, Butch and my dad, and Bill in back at the hunting lodge.

In between jobs, we continued to go to our hunting camp in Pennsylvania. When my brother Bill was on leave from the military and came for a visit, we'd always try to get everyone together to spend a weekend there. By then my brother Butch was working for Bell Telephone, installing lines. One time he slid off the pole and used his hands to stop himself from falling. Fortunately, he wasn't hurt, but he got a lot of splinters, some of which are still embedded in his hands.

My dad and I continued to work together, and we had several interesting drilling jobs. On one of them, we took the very first test borings for Co-Op City. Located in the Baychester section of the Bronx in New York City at the intersection of I-95 and the Hudson River Parkway, Co-Op City became the largest public housing development in the world. Early in the 1960s, the 320-acre area was home to a large amusement park called Freedom Land. It had animals, rides and roller coasters. The original concept for the theme park was American history, and it was laid out in the shape of a large map of the United States. But it quickly ran into money problems and went bankrupt.

By the time we arrived, the rides and roller coasters had been torn down and leveled, but some of the animals—wild buffalo, llamas and zebras—were still around, housed in their pens under tents. We were working for a company called Reliable Drilling that had a bunch of rigs there—at least six or seven. My dad was my helper and Donnie Grahamer was our foreman. He would provide us with gas, get us set up every morning and move us to another site when we were done.

Since the whole development would sit on landfill that used to be marsh land, we were drilling down to locate the bedrock. As a result of our findings, when construction started, the engineers extended the building foundations—50,000 concrete pilings for the high-rises—all the way down through the landfill. The rest of the development—roads, sidewalks, playgrounds, commercial buildings and garages—weren't anchored that way, so they keep developing cracks as the ground underneath continued to settle. In 2003, one of the parking garages partially collapsed and others were found to be unsafe, too. Altogether, Co-Op City ended up being 35 high-rise apartment buildings which house around 55,000 people, and at certain times of day, especially around sunset, the towers, which are separated by lots of green space, look like a futuristic city in a 1950s sci-fi movie.

My dad and I also did the original test borings on the first leg of the Washington Metro subway system in the District of Columbia. I don't remember how many rigs we had on that job. There may have been several other companies involved besides Giles Drilling. It wasn't unusual to share the work if it was a large enough job like this one.

We ended up drilling all over, working right on the streets and sidewalks. The police would set up barricades to prevent people from driving into our rigs or spectators from interfering with us. People are naturally curious and want to find out what's going on. Sometimes, we'd have to drill right in the middle of a street, and the cops would close off the whole block.

The consultants would tell us where to put the holes down, and we'd start off taking soil samples every foot and a half. Once we'd reached a certain depth, we'd go every 5 feet. On this job, the engineers were less interested in weight-bearing rock strata than in the make-up of the overburden. The composition of the soil would tell them what kind of machinery they would need to excavate the tunnels beneath the city.

City drilling presents unusual challenges because there is so much infrastructure—water, sewer and gas pipes, and electrical and telephone cables, which in some cases go back more than 50 years. Our engineers came prepared with all kinds of maps and did a good job of guiding us. We never hit anything during the weeks we spent there drilling.

I must say that I personally never did any severe damage throughout my career. I hit things driving casing and bent a few pipes in my day—by the time you start drilling for core samples, you're usually too deep to encounter anything man-made. But you keep checking the water from flushing the hole for what kind of shavings come out. That way you usually know when you've hit something and can stop right away.

But I know drillers that caused considerable damage. I remember hearing about one job where they put a drive-in theater out of business, and a number of subdivisions had to make do without electricity for a day or two because the drillers hit buried power lines. Gas and water lines are easy targets, too. When an accident happens, everything gets shut down, and you just sit back and wait until the utility company comes and fixes the problem you have created. It is part of doing business, and the drilling companies are insured against it.

One of my worst mistakes occurred when we were drilling for bridges and overpasses for Interstate 287. Once weekend I left my drill rig sitting on the right bank of the Raritan Canal in Piscataway, New Jersey, not paying attention to the weather forecast. Well, it rained hard that weekend and when the river overflowed, it covered the rig high enough to ruin the motor and put me out of commission. By Monday morning when I arrived, the waters had subsided, but the damage was done. I felt like a horse's ass having to call up the office and tell them what had happened. We had to get the rig carted to the yard to get it cleaned out and lost valuable time while I waited for another drill rig to be sent out before I could continue with the job.

Another time it was my carelessness that caused a serious accident. Donnie Grahamer and I were working alongside a railroad track—he was the driller and I acted as his helper. We had 15 feet of half-inch pipe strung together, and I was lifting it out of the hole with the cathead and asked Donnie to come over to help lay it down. There was water on the ground from flushing out the hole and as I lifted the pipe up, unbeknownst to me, it touched the high tension lines on the side of the tracks. When Donnie grabbed hold of the pipe, he got electrocuted. He was shaking like a dog spitting razor blades and kept saying, "Make it stop, make it let go!" I immediately threw the rope off the cathead and the pipe hit the ground. As it bounced, it hit Donnie in the chin and knocked him 20 feet away.

Me and Donnie Grahamer with a mobile drilling rig on a job.

We called an ambulance and rushed him to the hospital. Donnie had a deep cut in his chin, and the electrical current had made the nails in his shoes so hot and that they burned holes in his socks. Fortunately, he had gloves on, so his hands didn't get burned. I could have kicked myself—I should have been more careful and looked up to see that the wire was touching the pipe. It was one of the scariest times in my life. If I hadn't been able to throw the rope off right away, he probably would have been killed.

But Donnie didn't blame me and didn't hold a grudge. We partnered on a lot jobs, switching off as driller and helper. One I remember was Stewart Air Force Base in Newburg, New York, on the Hudson River, for new runways. We also did a lot of work for the expansion at Newark Airport.

The summer after Billy Hoffman finished college, we took test borings in the dry docks of the Norfolk Naval Ship Yards in Virginia, and he worked as a helper for us. It was great to spend time with him on the job and afterwards. At the time, the Navy was building the aircraft carrier Ranger, and I wanted to check it out. It wasn't top secret, but you had to have all kinds of clearance to get on it, so I put on my hard hat, acted like I knew what I was doing and just walked on and took a tour. I had never been on a navy vessel before, and although they had only finished the hull and deck, I was impressed by their massive size.

Donnie and I were like two brothers. We both liked to work hard, play hard and drive fast, sometimes to the point of being more than a little reckless. We both bought '62 Chevys when they first came out—blackwall tires, 327 engine, 4-speed on the floor, positraction rear end—identical except for the color. His was green and mine was almost pitch-black.

For one job on the Hudson River in New York, we got to park our cars in an empty warehouse. It had wooden floors and was three football fields long. Well, on our lunch breaks we'd race each other in there, fishtailing on the floors. When we came back from doing the subway in Washington, D.C., we went side-by-side over the Goethals Bridge that connects New Jersey and Staten Island. We must have been going 100 miles an hour. Another time, I drove like a maniac going down the New Jersey Turnpike. I had my dad and my brother Butch in the car. I get scared now just thinking about it—I was doing at least 120 miles an hour and could have wiped out half of my family.

Apparently, driving fast and recklessly was not uncommon among drillers. When my dad was working for the Erie Railroad in Armonk, New York, and driving home one weekend, he came upon a bad accident. He stopped and went to look. The car must have skidded out of control on the wet road and crashed head-on into the concrete pillar of an overpass—it was a heap of twisted metal and the driver and passenger were both so mangled that my dad didn't recognize them. It was only when he got home and heard about the accident from his neighbors that he realized that it was Tom Ritchie and Happy Jackson, two guys he had grown up with and known all his life. They had been coming from a drilling job and speeding to make good time, and it cost them their lives.

As I got older, I got tired of the life in the fast-lane, and I didn't enjoy the work as much as I did before. Although I was home more than when we had lived in Scranton, there were still too many weeks when I was too far away, and I missed Barbara, Shelly and Bobby. So I looked around for other possibilities, and when an opportunity came along, I decided it was time for a change and jumped at it.

Chapter 6
A NEW VENTURE

There had been some downtime between drilling jobs. It didn't happen very often, but when it did, I'd work for some of the local companies that drilled water wells in the New Jersey suburbs. I also spent time filling in at Acker Drilling, which manufactured drilling equipment in Clarks Summit, Pennsylvania. There I met Larry Defazio, who became a good friend and is now a member of our hunting club. At the time, he was the assistant to the vice president of the company and in charge taking photographs of the drill rigs, split spoons, rods and diamond bits, and creating brochures.

When one of the drillers at Haller Labs told me that the owner of April Well and Pump Company in Greenbrook, New Jersey, was looking for help, I went to see Dick Cleaves and applied for the job. Barb and I discussed it at length. Although I would be taking a hefty pay cut, we figured it was worth it. Greenbrook was only 5 miles from my house—no more long-distance traveling—and I'd be home at night. By then our kids were both in school and Barb had started to work again, which would make up for some of our loss in income. So when Dick offered me the job, I bit the bullet and said yes.

Dick teamed me with a fellow named Henry Sliwa. We'd load up every morning and go out for the whole day, putting in the pumps for water wells. Henry was a big, strong Polish fellow, and we got along very well. He reminded me of some of the guys I had grown up with in Scranton, although he had been born in Poland and hadn't come to the United States until he was around 20 years old. He had been 5 at the start of World War II and still remembered when the Nazis came marching into Warsaw, his home town and the nation's capital. As Henry's helper, I learned the ins and outs of pumps and wells quickly. Within a year, on weekends, I had my own part-time pump business on the side.

Dick Cleaves was a decent enough boss, but we were working 10 hours a day, six days a week, and after a couple of years, Henry and I finally got smart. Rather than bust our butts for someone else, we figured we'd be better off going into business for ourselves. So in 1969, we went to Clarks Summit, Pennsylvania, which is about 20 minutes north of Scranton off Route 81, and started Summit Well and Pump Company there as equal partners. I sold our home in Hillsborough and moved my family lock, stock and barrel. Henry and his wife, Marie, relocated, too; his son, Joey, had finished high school already and was working as a scuba diver for the Tennessee Valley Authority.

We bought a pickup truck and set up shop in a lumberyard where we rented office and storage space. Over the course of a year, we managed to get a few jobs, but we didn't make a dime. At some point, Henry and I held a strategy meeting and decided to move back to New Jersey before we went too far in the hole. We figured we couldn't do much worse, as we knew the area well.

We both rented apartments in Finderne Heights in the Bridgewater section of New Jersey. I lived on the second floor of the complex and Henry had his place across the courtyard. We kept the name Summit Well and Pump Company from where we'd gotten our start in Pennsylvania—there was a Summit, New Jersey, but it had nothing to do with us.

We set up our first shop in Possumtown in the garage of a house whose owners we knew well. After a slow start, things started to click, and we finally made some money. It was during the westward expansion of communities from New York, and most developments had no sewers or city water lines. Every single house would have its own septic system and water well and pump. When we made a good connection with a builder, we'd end up installing every pump in the new neighborhood. At times there were as many as 100 homes in one tract. Once the builders knew they could trust us to so a great job for a decent price, we'd get hired for their next big project, too.

We subcontracted the actual drilling and concentrated on pump installation. Early on, we hired the Assanti brothers, Mike and Lenny, and it turned out to be one of the best things that could have ever happened to us. Their company, an old, established outfit in Martinsville, had been started by their father. The Assantis had their own drill rigs and put in pumps, too. We hired them to drill the wells for the tract houses we were doing, and they, in turn, would give us their extra pump installation work.

Mike and Lenny were good people. They liked to hunt and fish, and they worked hard all their lives. Generous with advice, they were very helpful to Henry and me as we got started. No matter what questions we had, they'd sit down with us, share their expertise and give us a thorough answer without looking for anything in return. Later on, they were like an extra pair of fathers to my son, Bobby, when he came into our business.

Their generosity extended to other areas as well. There was a family that lived near an airport in Manville, New Jersey, whose well became contaminated with aviation fuel. They were very poor and could not afford anything new. Henry and I were the first on the scene. When we went to the Assanti brothers and told them about the situation, they drilled a brand-new well for them. And we put in the pump. The local Catholic Church raised some money through donations and paid us a token amount for our work, but the Assantis didn't want any of it.

A few years ago, Bobby and I bought them out. Not only did they come to work for us, but they brought their licenses with them. As a result, just sending them out on a job proved helpful to us. Lenny retired soon afterward and moved to Maryland. Mike worked for us full-time up until the recent recession before starting to cut back on his hours.

So Henry and I were fortunate when we got started. We had a fine partnership that lasted 20 years. In all that time, I don't think we ever had an argument.

At first, we worked like the dickens. We did so well that we were able to buy new homes after a couple of years in Bridgewater. Mine was right by the high school on Bayberry Road, and we stayed there the whole time for my children's primary and secondary education. My daughter, Shelly, owns it now—we sold it to her when Barbara and I retired to Florida. She lived there until she moved to the Sunshine State as well, and now rents it out.

The first year we also instituted a program for donating gifts to a needy family at Christmas. I will never forget the first person we helped, a black fellow in Piscataway, New Jersey. His name was Foster Moseley. He was in his fifties—older than us—lived alone and had lost one of his legs to diabetes. Henry and I donated a basket of food and some clothes for him. Occasionally, we'd go over to his house and sit with him and listen to him tell stories.

Barbara and I continued the program for as long as we lived in New Jersey. We had the Bridgewater Chief of Police, Dick Fetzer, identify the families in need for us. We'd buy mostly food and toys, in some cases bicycles and winter coats, and donate them anonymously—we didn't know the names of the recipients, and they didn't know ours. When I retired to Florida, Shelly, Bobby and his wife, Debbie, took over the program.

Installing pumps was a different kind of animal from drilling for core samples. You had to apply for a permit, and the regulations were somewhat different for each township. But the basic rule was that the well had to be 100 feet from the septic system (a tank in the ground or a septic field), which was in the back of the house most of the time, so we'd have to drill the well in front. How far in back the septic system was located determined how far the trench had to be from the well to the house—usually between 30 to 60 feet.

In those days, we didn't have a backhoe, so we had to dig the trenches by hand with pick and shovel. If the ground was hard, we'd use a jackhammer. We'd have to go a minimum of 3 feet deep to get below the frost line. After we'd finished the trench, we'd put down some straw or soft soil and lay twin plastic water pipes— one for the water and the other for the electric wires—and poke a hole in the side of the house to connect them up inside.

At first, we installed one of two types of water retrieval systems. In the jet system, the pump would be in the basement. Water would be forced down the hole through one pipe and up through another, creating continuous circulation—and the water for the home would be drawn from the constant flow. In the submersible system, the pump was down in the well below the water level and forced water up the pipe and into the house under pressure. In later years, just about all the systems we installed were submersible.

In the early days, the wells were much shallower and we didn't have to put so much casing in the ground. But in later years, we had to seal off the top water veins with concrete, so the water level would start deeper, and the wells had to be drilled farther down. Nowadays, most of the townships require installing 50 to 60 feet of steel well casing, regardless of whether rock is sticking out of the ground or starts 10 to 15 feet below the surface. In any case, you have to drill through the rock, put in the casing and seal it with concrete. That way you're sealing off any contamination that might be in the overburden or the top veins feeding the well. You continue to drill below until you've hit enough feeder veins to supply a domestic home with enough water. Then you install a pump, which forces the water into a pressure tank inside the house, usually in the basement.

In communities built on red shale, the wells might go 200 feet deep. But when there was granite, a much harder rock, the veins would carry less water, and the wells might have to go as far down as 500 feet and would only collect a few gallons a minute. Still, if there is a good water level in the well, it will be enough to take care of a family of three or four people.

The submersible pumps push water into a tank that had a pressure switch with a 20 pound differential. The pump might start when the pressure drops below 30 pounds in the tank and shut off at 50 pounds. That will be sufficient to bring water through the all faucets inside the house, flush the toilets and allow the people living there to run a bath or take a shower.

When Henry and I started off, there were companies that made pumps that lasted 20 years. Since then, the average life span has dropped, just as with cars, tires and refrigerators. When I retired from the business, the average life span was around 10 to 12 years. Of course, it depends a lot on how much water the family uses. The frequency and amount of starting and stopping determines the life of the pump.

You must have potable water, of course, so after we installed the system, we had to take a sample to the local board of health to get approval for the well. If the water didn't pass muster, we'd have to seal that well and drill another—it happened from time to time. When there was only a small amount of contamination, we were sometimes allowed to use some kind of filter system (ultraviolet light, iodine or reverse osmosis) to make sure the water was safe to drink.

Although I missed some aspects of core drilling, being my own boss more than made up for it. When I was working for someone else and burned up a diamond bit or bent casing, I'd feel guilty about costing the company owner money and taking away from his profit. But when it was my own business and I did something wrong, it was on my own head. For the most part, we didn't make a lot of mistakes—we did a lot better than weathermen or star athletes. I've always said that if I'd made as many mistakes on my jobs as baseball players do on theirs, and get paid what they do, I'd have had a life on easy street.

As I said, when Henry and I started out, we worked like the dickens. Eventually we got a helper, and as our business grew, we had helpers for both of us and a third crew going. We made it a practice to send a postcard a year to the day after we'd installed a pump, offering to service the system by checking the pressure and taking steps to increase the life of the pump. Often when we showed up, people would be out of the house running errands or picking up their kids from school. They'd leave the door open for us, and we'd do our job and leave the bill on the kitchen table. We had an excellent reputation for being trustworthy and doing a good job.

In many ways, the business became a family affair. My brother Butch helped dig trenches from time to time. Butch spent most of his career with telephone companies, first at New Jersey Bell, later with AT&T. Then he worked for us for a while, doing permits and delivering materials to drillers.

After my brother Bill retired from the Marine Corps, he spent some time in our employ, too, taking care of all the permitting. But when a position opened up in the Bridgewater Police Department, he became a cop. He was living in Warren Township then, and when it formed its own police department (the state police had patrolled it until then), he got a job as a police officer there. Later he moved to Las Vegas, Nevada, and worked in security for the Luxor Casino before finally retiring to Ingram, Texas, in the hill country south of San Antonio.

My wife, Barbara, did the books for us at night after she finished at Gavazzi Tires. In many ways, the business was Henry, Barb and I. Henry's wife, Marie, worked there part-time, too, but she was not as fully involved as the rest of us. On weekends, when I went out on a service call, Barb often came with me. She'd sit in the truck working on checks and bills while I installed or serviced a pump. It was a great way to spend time together, as it gave us a chance to talk during driving time.

Another regular from the old Scranton days who worked for us during the summers was Ken Rozelle. After a stint in the Navy, he'd become a physical education teacher in the Bridgewater school system. He was someone I never lost track of. Even after he left Scranton, I continued to hear stories about him, and I knew that he and his wife Jan had ended up in New Jersey, although I never dreamed that we would become such close neighbors and good friends again. When I moved to Bridgewater, he lived right up over the hill from me. We visited each other and went out to eat together many times.

Ken loved his job at Eisenhower Grade School and was much beloved as a teacher. He spent 35 years instructing most of the kids in the area, although Shelly and Bobby, who went to different schools, never had him. In some cases, he taught three generations of the same family. As a gym teacher, he was more of a father figure than a disciplinarian, but he knew how to keep his students in line. Soft-spoken, he could be gruff when necessary. He was truly one of the great, mild-mannered tough guys in my life.

Ken Rozelle.

Every summer, Ken would come to work for us at Summit Well and Pump Company. In those days, just about every teacher who had a family had to take a job during the two and a half months off to supplement his income. It was hard work and long hours, but we had a lot of fun times together. We never grew tired of kidding him about his last name—was he sure that he really wasn't related to Pete Rozelle, the former commissioner of the National Football League!?

Our company sponsored a lot of sports teams—girls' softball, legion baseball, little league, and adult teams. Ken Rozelle loved sports and, along with Butch, played softball on many of our adult Summit teams. When I wasn't at home cutting the lawn or doing painting around the house, I attended our children's athletic functions. I never missed any of Bobby's games or practices. He played Pop Warner football, and I was his coach.

From left: Bobby, Shelly, Bobby's best friend, Greg Adams, and my wife, Barbara, during a vacation on the New Jersey shore.

In high school, Bobby played quarterback on the football team and catcher during spring baseball. In his senior year, he was captain of both teams and was honored with the Joe Porcaro Award as outstanding athlete and scholar in his class.

Shelly was very active in softball and became a twirler in high school, so there were days when Barb and I, chauffeuring our children, had to head in different directions.

I must say, we had a great life, filled with work, friends and family activities and get-togethers on holidays. Business was good, and we were very much part of the community and enjoyed life to the fullest.

The only sad times came when my parents died. My dad had his first heart attack while working with Donnie Grahamer on a drilling job at Columbia University in New York City. He was 59 years old. Although he recovered, he could not do any heavy work after that. It was hard on him because he loved to be physically active. In the later years, he worked in bars. He and my mother lived in Daleville then, outside of Scranton in the country, and we spent holidays and many other occasions together. During our visits, Barbara and Dad loved to play cards for hours on end.

When he had a massive stroke in 1971 and died in the hospital, we were all very upset, although it did not come as a surprise because his health had been deteriorating.

My mom moved in with her mother and sister in Williamsport, Pennsylvania. In 1976, she contracted pancreatic cancer. We had an ambulance bring her to a hospital in New Jersey close to us, and she passed away soon after. We buried her in the Dunmore Cemetery alongside my dad and next to my sister, Janet, and my grandparents, aunts and uncles—the whole Kreilick clan.

Her death came as a shock to my brothers, my children and me, but it was especially hard on Shelly. She and my mom had been inseparable when she was younger. When she went shopping, Mom always took Shelly with her, driving in a Ford Falcon named Betsy—Shelly was her little girl.

I felt bad that both of my parents died too young. It didn't seem fair. They had worked hard all of their lives, giving their all to their children, grandchildren and friends, but they didn't get much of an opportunity to enjoy their golden years.

My dad and mom, Ray and Margaret Kreilick.

But life goes on.

When Shelly graduated from high school, she went to a work for a bank in Bridgewater. She lived at home for a while and then got her own condo in Bedminster, New Jersey. Later, she went to college in Doylestown to become a veterinarian—she loved animals, and we always had dogs. First there were two Scotties, Montgomery (my mother's maiden name) and Savannah. Then there was our first Westiem, Cricket, which was also the name of a boat I later had in Florida.

Shelly thought she would be working with animals, but during her freshman year she spent a lot of time grooming and polishing the nails of different dogs, as if to get them ready for the 4-H fair.

After the second semester, she had enough and quit. That's when she came to work for us, running the office, doing the books and taking care of collections. It's been her job ever since. Now that she is married and living in Sarasota, Florida, with her husband, Dave, she still is in charge of the office, long distance, but her day-to-day role has been much reduced.

When Bobby finished high school, he attended the University of Rhode Island, majoring in geology and oceanography. After he graduated in 1984, he came to work with us at Summit Well and Pump Company, starting out as Henry's helper and learning the business ground-up.

Five years later, when Henry decided to retire, Bobby bought out his share of the business and became my partner.

Chapter 7
A NEW SUMMIT

Although Bobby was not a driller by vocation, he had worked hard with Kenny Rozelle, Henry and me, and he also had a larger vision for the company. After he bought out Henry, he came to me and said, "Dad, why don't we buy a drill rig and get into the environmental drilling business."

I had my doubts. Our business was doing well, and we were quite comfortable. I was 45 years old. We had homes and fancy cars, we were doing what we wanted to and starting to relax. Why get involved in something that could take everything away from us? Besides, we didn't have an expert driller, and we would need someone we could trust.

A week or so later, I happened to have lunch with Donnie Grahamer. At the time, he was already working for an environmental drilling company in South Jersey, and I asked him flat out, "Donnie, if I buy an environmental drill rig, would you come to work for me?"

He didn't hesitate before saying, "Yes!"

So I talked it over with Barbara. Buying a drill rig would require a big investment and we'd be taking a great risk. It would almost be like starting a new business from scratch. But she said, "Let's do it," and we went ahead with it.

So we started Summit Drillling Company Inc. We purchased a large rotary drill mounted on a truck with big compressor. At the time, it cost around $60,000. The support truck that would follow it with all the necessary equipment and materials—sand, gravel, water—was another $30,000. I had quite a few sleepless nights as we went ahead and turned our decision into reality. In fact, every time we bought a new piece of equipment after that, it scared the bejezzus out of me.

When Donnie came to work for us, there was an immediate side benefit. He also started to drill our water wells, so we didn't have to subcontract those jobs anymore.

To begin with, most of our customers were oil companies (including Hess, Exxon, BP, and Shell) that had us work around their gas stations and tank fields.

Environmental drilling is quite different from the drilling Donnie and I had done for so many years when we had taken test borings and core samples. It basically means putting in a permanent well that allows the monitoring of contaminants in the ground. After drilling a hole to a certain depth, we'd install a PVC casing 2 to 4 inches in diameter with a screen on the bottom. Then we'd pack sand around it at the bottom. That allowed any contamination in the area to flow into the well and consultants to put their measuring equipment down to determine if there was gasoline or any other poisonous substance. When we were done, we would cover the well with a manhole.

The next time you fill your car up with gas, check out some of the manhole covers at the station. The ones that have a triangle on them are for the monitor wells. If you go to a landfill, look for any casing pipes that stick out. Those are monitor wells that check for methane gas and other contamination.

Since starting the company, we have drilled for pharmaceutical companies, at military bases, airports and many oil company installations. For one job, Hess Oil sent us to the island of St. Lucia. We actually transported one of our rigs there by ship. The crew took their wives with them and had a fine time combining business with pleasure.

In 1989, Greg Adams joined Summit Drilling Company. He had grown up in Bridgewater and was Bobby's friend all through high school. They went to college and roomed together at the University of Rhode Island. Greg then got a job at Seton Hall, and later at Princeton, which put him in charge of all the sports activities. At some point he sent us his resume—he wanted to come to work for us, and Barbara hired him on the spot. We knew his background, his family, his values and integrity. He soon became a very important part of our business, and as vice president and COO of our company, he is now Bobby's right-hand man.

When his dad died at an early age of a heart attack, Greg asked us to come to Maine with him to spread the ashes in a hunting camp he and his father had started there, and we were honored by his request. Greg, his wife, Mary Beth, and his three children have been like family to us. I am proud that he took me on almost as a second father, and we are still very close.

Under Bobby's leadership, Summit Drilling Company has taken off like gangbusters. As we expanded, we added other rigs as needed—small, big, air and auger rigs. We now have a fleet of 20 drill rigs. All of them have support trucks—warehouses on wheels that travel with them, carrying sand, gravel, and 1,200 gallons of water in the truck bed. Each rig has a team of two men (although Hess Oil requires three men on a rig at all times), and there is a sizeable office support staff. Our company has grown from a few employees to close to 60.

A few years ago, we sold the well and pump part of the business to Pat McInaw, a young man who was running it for us. He has kept the name, Summit Pump and Well Company, but it now is a separate entity.

There seems to be no letup in business, even during the current recession. We recently got the job to do all the environmental work for the new Trans-Hudson Tunnel going from Kearny, New Jersey, into New York. It is an $8.7 billion project of the New Jersey Transit Authority, and we will be doing all the environmental and geo-technical wells—the latter are small probes for soil and core samples.

When Bobby told me about landing the job and I congratulated him on it, he joked, "That's why I have been pulling my hair out."

And I said to him, straight-faced, "You don't have any hair."

Needless to say I am very proud of my son, my Superman. He's very good at the job. He's done things I couldn't or wouldn't have done. He's not afraid to take calculated risks, and they have paid off very well.

With business going well, Barbara and I realized one of our dreams and built a vacation log house. We had bought a piece of property on Cortese Road, no more than half a mile from the hunting camp my dad had built in 1943. The family after whom the road was named had lived in the area for three generations and owned a great deal of land. They had developed some of it through their contracting business. At some point, they decided to sell off some of their properties. The price was right, so Barbara and I bought two lots in a beautiful wooded section along the Delaware River. We told some of our friends about it, and Donnie Grahamer and his wife, Helen, bought land there, too.

The house we built was a two-story log home. It was custom-designed to our specifications and assembled from a kit that had been put together in Montana. The lumber, lodgepole pine, came from trees that had been in a forest fire. The blaze had stripped all the bark and killed all the bugs and vermin. It took a little more than 3 months to build on the concrete foundation we had prepared for the arrival of the Montana crew. Unlike my homes in the past, I didn't do any of the work myself. I even had the local well company drill the well and install the septic system.

Our log home on the Delaware River.

Barbara, on the other hand, was very involved in the process. She always had a knack for interior design, as does my daughter, Shelly. Barb decorated every home we ever had. She especially loved African decorations, and the finished log house reflected her tastes and vision. She was responsible for all the specifications and went to the lumberyard to pick out the blue pine covers for the kitchen cabinets herself. We had an antique wooden dresser she thought would look good in the rustic bathroom, so she had it converted it into vanity with two sinks in the top and matching wall mirrors.

The finished log home was a cozy 3-bedroom with a walk-in shower, no door. It had slate floors, a beautiful kitchen and a stone fireplace 20 feet tall that went all the way through the roof, with two more fireplaces outside. The stack was made from river rock. In the middle of the dining room-kitchen area stood a 10-foot high pine trunk (not decorative, but for decorative purposes). We had a bear rug on the floor in the living room. My son Bobby had killed the bear on one of our hunting trips at the camp, had it skinned and tanned, and gave it to my wife as a present. We also had the pelt of a large raccoon that I had shot, mounted and hung in the TV room.

Barbara in our log home.

Outside, a huge deck overlooking the Delaware River wrapped around the house. There was a hot tub, and I spent many an occasion relaxing in the churning water, even when there were 3 feet of snow outside.

We called our log home *Gemuetlichkeit*—the German word for comfort and hominess—and spent as much time there as we could. For Christmas and New Year's celebrations, we'd invite my son, Bobby, and Greg Adams and their families, and have a ball.

While we loved our log house, after we moved to Florida, we spent less and less of our time there, so we sold it to my son. He had it for nearly 20 years until recently, when he sold it and bought a piece of property in the Catskill Mountains.

In the meantime, Summit Drilling Company continued to prosper under Bobby's guidance and leadership. He did such a fine job that I decided to retire in 1989 at age 51 and take on more of a consultant role. As president and CEO of the company, Bobby keeps me informed. We still talk several times a week about how things are going, but he's perfectly capable of running the company on his own.

Bobby lives in Flemington, New Jersey, about 20 miles away from Bound Brook, where Summit Drilling is headquartered. As a successful businessman, he is quite involved in the community, sitting on the boards of a local bank and YMCA. His wife Debbie has her own interior design business. Since my daughter, Shelly, moved to Sarasota, they have taken over the program that Henry Sliwa and I started to help a needy family at Christmas time.

Bobby's second home in the Catskills is on a 40-acre property that has a lake on it. He goes up there both in the summer and winter. He likes to take his sons, Travis and Bradley, ice fishing on Lake Elko—he has all the equipment for it—and he has instilled his love for the outdoors in them.

When Travis came to visit me in Florida last year, we spent a day fishing in the Gulf of Mexico aboard the *Midnite Son* with

Captain Brian Martell. We did quite well, catching several medium-sized fish, but then Travis hooked into a monster barracuda. The fight lasted more than 15 minutes before he managed to land the 56-inch, razor-toothed fish. I had it mounted and shipped to him as a Christmas gift.

Travis with his catch.

Bradley is a junior in high school. His parents were pleased to name him, but I would have named him "Storm." You see, Brad was born during the "storm of the century," in 1993. When the blizzard was heading toward New Jersey, Bobby and Debbie, 8 and a half months pregnant, figured they'd ride it out closer to the hospital in Barb's and my house in Bridgewater. And what a storm it was! Over the next 3 days, the blizzard dumped more than 3 feet of snow on the entire Northeast. When Brad decided it was time to be born, Bobby tried to get Debbie to the hospital in our four-wheel-drive Chevy, but the snow was coming down so hard and fast that they were unable to get out of the driveway. I called 911, and the chief of police himself and an ambulance arrived to save the day. I watched them drive off into the blizzard thinking all was okay. I found out later that the ambulance slid off the road into a huge snow bank. It took a rescue team to winch it out. The entire caravan finally arrived at the hospital and Bradley, aka "Storm," came into this world.

Brad and I recently teamed up for a fantasy football league. We named our team The Stingers. I was the acting owner, and Brad became the coach. We managed to squeeze into the playoffs as the 8th and final seed. Brad made some nifty trades, picked up a few players from the waiver wire, and we were on our way. In our very first year in the Sunday's Hero Fantasy Football League, The Stingers were crowned champs! It was great fun, and Brad and I look forward to next year.

Travis, Bradley, Bobby and Debbie.

Chapter 8
EARLY RETIREMENT

It took all of 15 minutes for me to get used to retirement.

Barb and I had been vacationing on Florida's West Coast for some time and loving it, so we decided to become snowbirds. We bought a townhouse in Fairway Bay on Longboat Key, one of Sarasota's main barrier islands in the Gulf of Mexico. It was a beautiful neighborhood. Walter Payton, the great Chicago Bears running back, lived only two blocks away.

When we first moved there, Barbara and I liked to go out to eat on St. Armands Circle. It was a novelty for us, and we especially liked the Columbia, a Cuban restaurant, and Café L'Europe, a 4-star French restaurant.

Barbara and I loved to go boating and fishing, so I bought a 32-foot Sea Ray Sun dancer, and named it *Summit*. It was a beautiful boat with twin engines—inboard-outboard—and two sleeping berths, with a full kitchen below deck. We spent many a night and weekend there and had a lot of fun on the water.

On several occasions, we also traveled to other Florida Gulf Coast vacation spots for special fishing trips.

One such excurssion took us to Ft. Myers and Sanibel Island, where our fishing guide was a personable, fun-loving Floridian named Randy Wayne White. That was before he became a well-known writer of mysteries featuring marine biologist-CIA agent Doc Ford. Our first outing was nearly 20 years ago, and I am happy to say I have enjoyed reading every one of his novels as much as spending time on the water in his boat. The books sit on a special shelf in my house, and a number of them are first editions and autographed by Randy himself.

One time, my son, Bobby, came for a visit and we went fishing with Randy as our guide. When Bobby caught a tarpon, Randy shut off the engine—he had a 28-foot Shamrock boat then—and we just sat there watching Bobby fighting the fish. It was 90 degrees, and Randy and I just sat there laughing, having beers and telling stories, while Bobby worked up a sweat. From time to time we'd get up and pour water over him to cool him down.

After a while Randy said to Bobby, "If I were you, I'd move the rod to one side."

When you're fighting a tarpon, you don't want to continue to hold the rod in front of you because when the line grows weak and breaks, the recoil will knock you in the head—hard—and you'll end up with a big bump.

Bobby took Randy's advice, and kept on battling—my son is a fighter. It took him a couple of hours to reel the tarpon in, which ended up weighing 165 pounds.

One of the great pleasures of coming to the Florida Gulf Coast was being able to reconnect with a number of old friends who had retired here before me. My former partner, Henry Sliwa, and his wife, Marie, lived in an apartment on the Ringling Causeway that links Sarasota and Lido Key, one of the bayfront islands, and we often went to St. Armands Circle together for a bite to eat or to have a drink.

Ken Rozelle and his wife, Jan, had moved to Venice, a small community just half an hour's drive to the south of Sarasota. When I got down here, we hooked up again. We'd go out to eat, and I watched him played softball, which he did at least three times a week until he was around 70. He died a few years ago, and I really miss him.

After Ken passed away, Billy Hoffman, Mickey, my daughter, Shelly, and her husband, Dave, and my friend Donna and I would go with Jan out once a month, but lately we haven't kept up the routine. Shelly still corresponds with her by email, though, and keeps me informed about what her kids, Renee and Casey, are doing. When they were growing up, I was like an uncle to them.

Renee went to college at Notre Dame, knew all the football players there, dated one of the starting linebackers and graduated with Joe Montana, the legendary quarterback for the San Francisco 49ers. She now lives in Dallas, and like me, is a die-hard Cowboys fan. When Casey attended Bridgewater West in New Jersey, the same high school as Bobby, he was one heck of an athlete, playing tight end on the football team, and I went to see every one of his games. He then attended college at Virginia Tech and now lives in California. Renee and Casey were like a part of my family.

I was delighted when Billy Hoffman and Mickey retired to Skidaway Island outside of Savannah, Georgia, because it meant that we were close enough again to visit each other more frequently. Whenever they spent time with us on Longboat Key, we'd lobby for them to buy a house here, and they finally did. Billy also built a beautiful log home in Maggie Valley, North Carolina, overlooking the Smokey Mountains, and he and Mickey make it their home during the summers.

Barb got very involved volunteering at Mote Marine Laboratory, a research facility and aquarium on the southern tip of Longboat Key. She especially loved working with dolphins.

While Barb and I lived in the townhouse, we met Emmitt and Linda Weber, who were big-time realtors and fellow boating enthusiasts. We took trips together to Key West on their yacht, a 40-foot Sea Ray.

At that time, there were still many empty lots in the Bayou, a beautiful neighborhood on the Sarasota Bay side of Longboat Key. One of them was a piece of property that I liked very much. It belonged to Chuck Savage, the owner of a 7-11 and a hardware store in the middle of the island.

I remember going down there one day to have a look, and Emmitt just happened be there, too. He was standing on the corner of the lot.

I asked him, "Is it still for sale?"

He said, "Yes."

And I bought it that day for $259,000.

We sold our townhouse and had Gary Roberts of Bamboo Homes build a brand-new home for us on our new lot. Once again, Barbara took an active part in all spects of its design. She and Gary would sit around the drafting table and discuss the ground plan, the interior and exterior looks, and the amenities. At times, they got into some spirited arguments, but in the end, we all were very satisfied with the results.

We parked our 32-foot Sea Ray Sun dancer in the Longboat Mooring Marina and were delighted to become a part of the social scene there.

When you move to Florida, a lot of people up north are happy to come visiting to enjoy the sunshine, especially during the winter months to escape the cold, clammy, grey weather. As it happened, when Greg Adams and his wife, Mary Beth, stayed with us, the Mooring Marina was building a new complex, and we were invited to participate in the groundbreaking ceremonies. We all went, and a picture of us wearing hard hats and holding shovels appeared in the local newspaper the next day.

Greg Adams took this picture of me and Barb in the center, and his wife, Mary Beth, on Barb's left. The rest are visitors from Canada.

In those early retirement days, Barbara and I still spent considerable time up north each year, especially during the summer months when Florida became an unbearably humid sweatbox and the climate at our lodge home on the Delaware River was more temperate and pleasant. Of course, we attended all important family functions and were delighted to no end when Bobby and Debbie got married. But in time, we found ourselves enjoying the Sunshine State more and more.

My son, Bobby, and Barbara at his weddding in New Jersey.

During our 10-year stay in our first house on the Bayou, Barbara and I met a lot of great people in our neighborhood and at the Moorings. Barb was wonderful at organizing parties, and we had quite a number of get-togethers, both at our house and in some of the nightspots on Longboat Key.

One of our favorite watering holes was The Buccaneer. Unfortunately, it's gone now, having made way for condo buildings.

One time when Bobby and his wife, Debbie, came for a visit, we went there for supper. Afterwards, they went to the lounge and met Ralph Shannon, a Country and Western singer who had toured with Eddie Arnold for 20 years. He'd settled in Sarasota and had his own restaurant on the Tamiami Trail. That night, he was performing, and we all thoroughly enjoyed it. Ralph and his wife, Beverly, became good friends, and Barb became the president of his local fan club. We'd go to The Buccaneer at least once a week—often more—to hear Ralph sing and play his banjo and guitar, and we followed him to other local venues as well. I still go to hear him sing from time to time at bars and the Shriners.

The other hangout was Schenkel's, which was owned by Edith Barr, who wore cowboy hats and would sing at the bar. She later sold the place and it became The Poseidon for a while before it got torn down to make way for residential houses.

I didn't play golf until I was in my late 40s. In New Jersey, we'd had all those softball teams we sponsored, so we didn't bother with hitting a little white ball with clubs. But when we started to come to Florida, I took up golf and found it to be a most enjoyable game, and by far the most frustrating sport I have ever played. What I lack in finesse, I make up for with strength, following the advice Billy Hoffman once gave me, "Hit the ball hard. It's got to go somewhere."

Barbara and I played together a little, but she didn't get into the game until we moved to Florida for good. She played at the Long Boat Key Club, just a stone's throw from where we lived on the Bayou. Although she was not an athlete, she quickly got the hang of it. I bought her a used set of clubs, and she took lessons, practiced and soon came to love the game. She did well in a couple of tournaments and became 9-hole champion at the Long Boat Key

Club two out of three years. She had her name in the newspapers more than me!

Once, when there was a PGA tournament at the Bent Tree Country Club, we went to see the women pros on the tour play. I ended up sitting on the grass with a group of people that included the husband of Nancy Lopez, Ray Knight, the ex-baseball player, who won the 1986 World Series with the New York Mets. When people asked to see his championship ring, Ray took it off and passed it around. I tried it on my finger. I don't remember if Nancy won that tournament, but I do know that ring was so big, it all but covered my finger.

Golf brought us into contact with a lot of interesting people, many of whom became our friends. It also is the reason I made one the worst mistakes in my life. There were two female teaching pros at the Longboat Key Club, and they introduced us to a movie producer who was planning to make a film about Tiger Woods, starring Samuel Jackson. He was looking for investors. A number of our friends thought it was a good idea, and after Barb and I talked about it, we contributed $50,000 to the project. Well, the producer turned out to be a crook and he was running a scam that took in a lot of people. We never got a dime back from the money we'd invested, but we did get back at him. We tracked him down and had him arrested. He ended up serving three years in jail.

When Barb played golf with her friends, she'd take our Navigator, pile six to eight women inside (or they'd take a couple of vehicles), and go somewhere over night. They'd shoot a round of golf, play cards, have drinks—Barbara's favorite was Bacardi Light Rum and Coke—and indulge in chocolate deserts. Barbara had a soft spot for Reese's peanut butter cups and was quite capable of putting away a whole bagful in the course of an evening.

But those excursions, our fishing trips in Florida, and occasional visits up north were the extent of her travels. She was more of a homebody. But she encouraged me to travel whenever I wanted to, and I took her up on it and went to a lot of different places.

I'd go to our hunting camp in Pennsylvania every year for a week in the fall and try to make at least two other meetings.

Another time, I took a trip hunting and fishing in Alaska with Dyke Howell and Dan McFadden. I had met Dyke through boating at Longboat Key and played golf with him a number of times. He and Dan had been partners in a tunnel construction company called Frontier/Kemper, and they had both retired after selling the business to a German outfit. We flew to Alaska and went on a trawler that became our motel. We had two guides along, and we cooked all our meals and slept there. Except for our hunting and fishing excursions, we didn't leave it for the next three weeks.

We first went hunting for black bears. The trawler had two skiffs, and every morning two of us hunters would go out—we each had a guide—while the other two stayed on the trawler. If we spotted a bear on the beach, we'd go ashore, trying to stay downwind and track it. When we got close enough for a shot, we'd take it.

It was late one evening when I finally had my bear in sight and pulled the trigger, I knew I hit it, but it lumbered off the beach into the forest. My guide followed it, but had me stay with the skiff. You don't leave the beach in Alaska unless you know what you're doing, especially at 10:30 at night, because the forests are dense with fallen trees and treacherous holes. Also, the bay had 20-foot tides, so I had to make sure the skiff remained in at least a foot of water, or we would have been stranded for the next 12 hours—we were a good 20 miles from the trawler. When my guide returned, he said he had found blood at a place where the bear had rested, but by then it was so late that we decided to come back in the morning.

When I returned with both guides the next day, they located another spot where the bear had lain down, but there was no hide or hair of it. Perhaps another animal took it, or it dragged itself away—I'll never know.

Although I returned empty-handed, Dyke, Dan and our fourth companion each bagged a black bear. Our guides skinned them and we took the hides with us. In Alaska, the law says that you can leave the carcass because there is no waste. Eagles, wolves and other bears will clean it up in a very short period of time. In fact, when grizzlies and brown bears hear a shot, they will move towards it, knowing that something is being hunted and looking for an easy meal. It has happened that a hunter shot a 300- to 500-pound black bear, only to see a 1,200-pound grizzly come by and carry it off.

For our third week, we went fishing out of Petersburg in the inlets and coves of Glacier Bay Park, and I made up for striking out with my bear by catching a 120-pound halibut. In some of the bays, the waters are 300 feet deep, so you need a weight the size of a baseball on your rod to take the bait down to the bottom. Halibut can get to be as big as a Volkswagen and weigh 500 pounds—you try to pull a fish like that up from that far down, and you've got your work cut out for you.

All in all, we had a splendid time, but there was a sad follow-up. About three years ago, Dyke and Dan went to a reunion in Colorado with the German company that had bought them out. One of the highlights of the weekend was a trip into an abandoned mine. Dyke was not feeling well because of serious carousing the night before and had declined to come along. Dan and two German executives stepped onto the elevator platform that would take them down the shaft. A few feet into their descent, one of the lines got caught on the side of the shaft, tipping the elevator platform at a 45-degree angle. With nothing to hold on to, all three men plunged 500 feet to their death. The tragedy made national news, and Dyke came back badly shaken. As will happen with male friends, some wags kidded him that excessive drinking wasn't a bad habit, after all, trying to bring him out of his funk with gallows humor.

Dyke continues to hunt and fish—he's been on safari in Africa at least seven or eight times—and he introduced me to alligator hunting.

In Florida, you join a lottery and if you're picked, you receive a permit to hunt for a certain number of gators. When I started out, you could bag five, so you'd bring along a number of friends, but it has since dropped to two. At one point, I went 5 years in a row on Lake Okeechobee and other promising venues. One year our guide was Kendal Wilson, a 6 foot 6 inch tall, 300-pound giant, and we stayed at his father's house near the lake—our headquarters.

We hunted all night hunt from sundown to sunrise in as many as six or seven airboats—two men per boat. You were not allowed to use a rifle, only a crossbow or harpoon, which we made ourselves from 2-inch dowels 10 to 12 feet long with points held on by duct tape. We'd locate the gators by their red eyes, which were visible above the water as they rested on the water's surface in the lake. You can judge their size by the distance between the eyes. If it was big enough, we'd strike them with the harpoon, which had a 20-foot rope with a 5-gallon bucket and a Clorox jug attached at the end. The gator would dive and we'd follow and slowly pull it to the surface. Then we could use a bang stick that had a 45-caliber bullet or shotgun shell at the end to hit it in the head and, hopefully, stun it enough to be able to pull it alongside, tape its mouth shut and pull it aboard. Then we'd take an ax and sever its spinal cord. It's a gruesome business—not for people with weak stomachs—and you have to be careful, because the gator will thrash around.

That trip I bagged a 12-and-a-half-foot alligator. When we took it to the processor, I got 55 pounds of meat from the tail and had the head mounted. The processor gets the rest, that's the deal. Another time, I got an 8-footer, and both heads are on display in my study. I haven't hunted in about 5 years, but it is a lot of fun, and not much can compare with the rush when you take an alligator into your boat.

Kendall Wilson and me with my gator.

At some point, I joined the Gator Creek Golf Club, a private men's club on the Bee Ridge Road extension past I-75. The club has about 250 members, and pro golfers like Paul Aizinger have practiced there. The club has a number of former professional athletes as members. I've met Don Robinson from the Los Angeles Dodgers and Mike Levallier, the former catcher for the Pittsburgh Pirates. I've had the opportunity to play with Carlton Fisk, the catcher for the Boston Red Sox, who is now in the Baseball Hall of Fame, and Dicky Betts, the guitarist for the Allmand Brothers Band. Billy Hoffman joined, too, as did a number of my friends from Longboat Kay and St. Armands, notably Steve Sundheimer and Dyke Howell.

A number of the players I met there became good friends. A few of us joined together and founded a group called the ROMEOs, which stands for Retired Old Men Eating Out. The group includes Steve Sundheimer, Dave Smith, a pilot who flew for Delta Airlines for 35 years; Jack Feily, an ex–New York City fire fighter; John Knowles, a retired insurance broker; and Joe Patrick, who used to work for the Port Authority in New York City. Jack, John and Joe, along with their partner Jim Sullivan, are the owners of Patrick's Restaurant on the corner of Main Street and Pineapple, known as Five Points in downtown Sarasota, which has been voted to have the best hamburger in town for many years running. They also own three taverns in New York, all called The Piper's Kilt. They have restored one of them to its original décor, and it is often used for movie and television shoots. Another member is Phil McGowan, a realtor in town. He is a bit younger than the rest of us and an honorary ROMEO—not yet retired.

The ROMEOs have lunch once or twice a week, frequenting different restaurants around town, but Patrick's is the main gathering place, of course, because of its owners. We talk about our health and sports—some of the guys know more than many a sports writer—and solve the problems of the world. Well, somebody has to do it, after all. We've been meeting regularly for more than 15 years now. It's not always the same group, but whoever happens to be in town and available. Above all, they're good friends of mine, and they take good care of me.

Barb and I thoroughly enjoyed the years we lived at our house in the Bayou, but I always said I wished we had a garage. I had bought a vintage '57 Chevy—ivory and aqua-colored with white-wall tires—and I had to keep parking it with friends. So when a realtor told me that there was a house for sale down the street with room for five cars underneath, I was immediately interested.

Barb and I went to take a look and talk to the owner, who had just gotten divorced and was suffering from cancer. He was asking $1 million for the house—the deal of the century! Barb loved the upstairs and the large kitchen. She immediately had ideas about how to decorate it, and we decided to go for it. I was able to sell our old home at a profit, and we moved in a few months later.

Me, Shelly, Barb and Dave.

In 2001, we were delighted to attend our daughter's wedding in New Jersey when she got married to Dave Smith, a computer wiz whom she met when he set up the computer network at Summit Drilling Company.

Everything seemed to be going so well for us, and then disaster struck. I was flying back from a week at the hunting camp in Pennsylvania. It was a Continental flight direct from Newark to Florida. When I arrived in Sarasota and walked toward the exit past the Mote Marine exhibit in the upstairs lobby, I was greeted by Johnelle Smith, an ex-girl friend of Bobby's from high school who had become a doctor and was now living in Largo, Florida, with her husband, Pal, who is also a doctor, and her children, Jeremy and Jenna.

I said, "Where's Barb?"

Barbara used to like to play tricks on me. She'd be sitting at the bar with her back to the outside having a cocktail so I'd believe she wasn't there to meet me. We had been playing this game with each other for 40 years whenever we travelled.

But Johnelle looked serious and told me that Barbara was in the hospital and that things didn't look good. We didn't even stop to get my bags. We just got in her car outside and headed right for Sarasota Memorial Hospital.

Apparently, Barbara was to have coffee with Bill and Lena Seagrave, our friends and neighbors who lived down the block in the Bayou. Barbara was always on time, so when she didn't show up, Lena grew worried and went over to our house. We used to leave the screen door locked but kept the sliding doors between the bedroom and the lanai open. Lena called for Barbara, but there was no answer.

I don't know if she cut the screen door herself or went next door Chris Neisler, who owns Ringling Cleaners. In any case, they opened the door, went inside and found Barbara lying unconscious on the bed. They called an ambulance and rushed her to the hospital.

In the meantime, they also called Bobby and Shelly in New Jersey. Shelly got in touch with Johnelle, who agreed to meet me at the airport—Largo is about an hour or so north of Sarasota—and that is how she showed up when I got off the plane.

When we got to the hospital and talked to the doctors, they told us it was too late. Barbara had suffered a massive brain aneurism and there was nothing they could do.

The rest of the time was an anguished blur for me. While we were still at the hospital in the afternoon, Bobby and Shelly showed up—somehow they'd gotten a flight right away. How they managed it so quickly is still beyond me.

Since I was in shock and functioning as if I were in a dream, a terrible nightmare, Bobby took over. When we went back to our house, he had Steve Sundheimer come over and take all the guns out of my house. After we'd talked things over, Bobby made all the arrangements with the funeral home to have Barb cremated. He and Shelly coordinated all the people who had to come down from New Jersey.

Barbara died on December 8, 2002. I don't remember the funeral, but afterword we went out on Bill Seagrave's big Sea Ray. From where we lived in the Bayou to get into Sarasota Bay, you had to navigate through Buttonwood Harbor, a small inlet cove. It was there that we had a little ceremony. The group included Bill and Lena Seagrave, Steve Sundheimer and his wife, Lori, and my family—Bobby and Debbie, and Shelly and her husband, Dave. After everyone said a few words, we strewed Barbara's ashes into the waters of Buttonwood Harbor, the way she would have wanted it.

I haven't shed many tears in my life, but with Barbara's death I was emotional for a long time. She and I were married for 44 and a half years, and to lose her the way it happened, and me not being there, kept hurting and gnawing at me. I felt that God had betrayed me and I was angry at Him for quite some time. There were some days when I felt so bad, I just wanted to curl into a ball and not hear or see anyone.

During that bitter, painful time, Steve Sundheimer and his wife, Lori, were my lifeline. They invited me over to their house for supper every night for months. He told me early on, "Whatever we cook, we'll make three." He loved pork chops, and sure enough, whenever they were on the dinner menu, there was an extra one for me. Without him and Lori, I don't know what would have happened to me.

Steve is 70 and had open heart surgery a few years ago. I asked him at some point at one of our ROMEO lunches, "You're not smoking anymore, are you, Steve?"

And he said, "No."

But John Knowles, who was with us, said, "Steve, you were sneaking cigarettes."

Barbara always kept two packs of cigarettes in a drawer, and Steve, who knew that, used to come over to have a smoke, both before and after she died. John spilled the beans on him.

Another person who helped me during that dark period was Cynthia Craig. She is a massage therapist, and I had met her when Barbara had given me a massage from her as a present to help my back, which stiffens up from time to time ever since I injured it during the drilling job for the World Trade Center. Over the years, a number of people have given me such presents, and I thank them all. While Cynthia works primarily through the body, she is also a very spiritual person, and our conversations, during which she encouraged me to go on with my life, allowed my soul to begin to heal. Cynthia and I became good friends, and I still see her and her husband, Dr. Homayoun Bidabadi, socially to enjoy each other's company.

In time, I recovered like a sick man from a long illness. There are still days when I miss Barbara a lot and feel awful. We had a wonderful relationship. I can't think of anything we ever had a knock-down-drag-'em-out argument about. We discussed everything important to us and our family ahead of time—things we bought, times to move and things to do.

From time to time, I visit her. When I still had my boat, I'd go out to Buttonwood Harbor and take some Bacardi Light, a Reese's peanut butter cup and a Parliament cigarette, and throw them in the water.

We went out one time when Bobby was here for a visit, and wouldn't you know, a dolphin, the animal she loved most of all, came up and jumped out of the water in the bay right where she is buried.

We had asked people to donate money to Mote Marine in lieu of flowers at the funeral, and we bought a beautiful, large tank for the laboratory with a plaque: "In Memory of Barbara Kreilick."

Barbara and Dallas.

Chapter 9
OLD AND NEW FRIENDS

Hard as it is to lose someone so special, I got through it with a lot of help from my family and friends. I am very fortunate to have good friends who stood by me and made me comfortable.

They encouraged me not to jump at anything hurriedly, and I took their advice. I stayed in the house in the Bayou for another two years.

Sports and fishing trips helped take my mind off what had happened, too.

I had met Matt Zito on the Longboat Key Club golf course, and we'd become good friends. A retired architect, he had designed a house for Stuart "Stewie" Bitterman, a friend of Barb's and mine in New Jersey. When Stewie came to Florida, he sold that house to Whitney Houston and moved to Longboat where Matt designed his retirement home as well. Matt and his wife, Carol, have a place in Durango, Colorado, and I regularly go to visit them on my trips out West. They have two sons: Glen, a golf pro, and Jeff, a shock jock at a radio station—the Howard Stern of Naples!

In any case, I soon found out that Matt loves to go fishing, and we explored a number of places in Florida—Boca Grande, Sanibel and the Florida Keys. Bobby, Matt, Glen and I took a trip to Belize for tarpon and bonefish. Belize has the second largest barrier reef in the world—after Australia—but the fishing there was not as good as in the Keys. The bonefish aren't as big, and we caught only a couple of small tarpon.

Bobby and me with a 140-pound tarpon in Boca Grande.

In Marathon, just the other side of the Seven Mile Bridge, or out of Islamorada or Key West, the tarpon and bonefish are a challenge. Bone fish—one of the game fish everyone wants to catch—probably are, pound for pound, one of the best fighting fish on the planet. Bobby and I also caught a couple of large permit—flatfish that can get as big and round as a large manhole cover. When they're feeding, they dive like a duck in water with their heads down and their tails out, and they stir up the mud and sand, which is how you see them and catch them. We took them to a restaurant on the key, where they cook them up in different ways for an excellent meal.

Another time I traveled with Bobby, Matt and Jeff Collins, a friend I had met through Steve Sundheimer, to Costa Rica, and we went sailfishing in the Pacific Ocean right around the corner from Panama, We were 17 miles from shore, and we caught 17 or so sailfish and lost about as many. We had a ball. It was probably one of the best fishing trips I've ever been on. I ended up with a great souvenir, a 165-pound sailfish, six and a half feet long, that I caught, had mounted and hung in my study.

Me and my 165-pound sailfish.

I enjoy spending time with my son and friends on these trips. When you go away with a bunch of guys fishing for a couple of day, it's a lot of fun. You're out on in the sun on the water, heft a few beers and tell stories. Then you catch a tarpon, and if you manage to reel it in, you don't want two in a row. They're too exhausting. After you fish all day, you take a shower, go out to eat and maybe play cards afterwards.

I also played a lot of golf with my son. He is a good golfer. I've personally witnessed him getting two holes-in-one!

I, on the other hand, manage to do just okay. In those days I had a 19-20 handicap, which came in handy when I played in tournaments, especially in team competitions. Billy Hoffman and I often paired up. He being a very good golfer and me having a big handicap was a great combination—he's a good player and I got a lot of strokes.

Bill Hoffman and me on the golf course.

About five years ago, in one of the Gator Creek member/member tournaments, we won our flight. There were eight teams in each flight and seven flights altogether. The winning teams went back to the 9th hole and played a sudden-death round. Me, being a higher handicap player, got what they call "a stroke on the hole," an extra shot. Everyone teed off—14 guys on the same hole—and soon the fairway and the rough next to it were littered with golf balls. The golf pro followed us around and designated whose ball was farthest away from the green. That person went next.

I was fortunate to hit my first ball straight-away down the middle of the fairway. But my second shot veered off to the right of the green and ended up in a muddy area on a downslope that had no grass at all. Billy hit his second shot right onto the green. The other team with a high handicap was Carl Doty, and his partner Mike Cohen. Carl also got a stroke, and his ball was lying right next to Billy's, so he was in great shape to win the tournament.

As the player farthest from the hole, I got to hit next. I couldn't see the green or the hole, just the top of the flag. I used a sand wedge and did a chip shot—skulled the ball. I never saw it, but I'm told it just cleared the edge of the green, skimmed the top of the grass and made a beeline for the flagpole, where it hit the back of the cup and fell in the hole, breaking the plastic liner in the process. With my extra stroke, I had a three for two.

Well, all hell broke loose. There were guys lined around the green, lined up on the porch of the clubhouse—more than a hundred—watching, and they held up their drinks and cigars and started to hoot and holler, "It went in! It went in!"

Mike Cohen yelled over the din, "We still have a shot. Shut up!" But the best he and his teammate could do was to tie us, which would mean we'd be playing another hole.

Billy, being farther from the hole than Carl Doty, picked up his ball.

Carl looks at him and said, "What are you doing? You've got to put."

Bill shook his head. "No, I don't. My partner's in the hole with a three for two, so why should I putt and show you the line?"

That's the rule. When Carl went to put, he was so shaken up, he only made it halfway to the hole. Carl became so irritated he never went back into the clubhouse. He headed directly for his car and went home.

And Billy and I were victorious—we had won the tournament. It was the biggest thrill of my golfing career.

Mike Cohen and I still play together at the Laurel Oaks golf course. He's become good-natured about that loss and still kids me from time to time, "If I'd had a gun that day, I'd have shot you!"

In the meantime, I had recovered enough to start going out again. I said, "Yes," when people invited me to parties. At night, I'd head to the bars at Hemingway's, Tommy Bahama's or 15 South on St. Armands Circle.

There was a woman named Donna Dolan who also lived in the Bayou. Her husband had died about a year and half earlier of a stroke. I had seen her walking her dogs—at that time she had a border collie and a dog that looked like Old Yeller—but I had never talked to her.

Well, one evening someone was having a party and wanted me to meet her. I happened to have a date that night, and I brought my daughter, Shelly, and Johnelle Smith who is a dead ringer for Jennifer Lopez, along with me, so when I walked in and was introduced to Donna, I had three beautiful women on my hip, so to speak. Donna and I did have a conversation later that evening. We laughed about my entrance, but nothing came of our talk.

Some days later when I saw Donna walking her dogs—I was looking for her now—I stopped her and asked if she would go out with me to a movie and a bite to eat, and she said, "Yes." We hit it off well and started to see each other more often. We'd go out to restaurants and she invited me to her house for dinner.

She is a beautiful woman and great mother. She wasn't always down here, because she and her son Tim jointly own a wholesale giftware business in Columbus, Ohio, with reps in four states, selling items to Hallmark stores and hospital gift shops, and she periodically travels back up north and to tradeshows. Tim has a wife, Heidi, and an 11-year-old son, Jack. Donna's younger son, Scott, is a Vice President of Operations for United Airlines in charge of baggage, ticket counters and getting the planes off the ground. He has 16,000 people working for him, a big job with a tremendous amount of responsibility. His companion, Kim Marsella, is a sweet, vivacious young woman, and they have been going together for seven years.

When we got together, we enjoyed each others' company, so about two months later, I asked Donna to come on a trip to Australia with me.

We flew to Hawaii and from there to Sidney. The tour was organized by Abercrombie and Kent, and we had our own guide and driver. We drove into the outback for a week and stayed at a number of beautiful ranches.

At one of them, we went horseback riding. I was wearing a snazzy western hat, and when I got on the horse, Heidi, the girl that acted as our guide said, "I think I finally found my cowboy."

When the ride was over, my horse wanted to go with the other horses. As we headed under a pine tree with low boughs, I put up my arms to stop and went ass over tin cups, falling to the ground.

We quickly determined that I wasn't hurt, at which point our girl guide said, "And tomorrow, we'll practice Bob's way of dismounting a horse." We all had a good laugh over it.

One morning we walked all the way around Ayer's Rock. It was too hot to take the trip to the top. A park ranger, a pretty young woman, picked us up at 4 a.m. and led us on the 7-mile hike through sand and over red rock. She pointed out the caves and other places that are off-limits to tourists because they are sacred ground for the Aborigines. At one point we were surprised to see a camel, and our guide explained that camels were brought to Australia at some point and now run wild there. Halfway around the rock we stopped for breakfast, and then continued on so we could finish the hike and make it back to our hotel before it got too hot.

That night we had a supper under the stars, and an astronomer was on hand to tell us about all the constellations and the Milky Way. That far away from civilization, there are no lights that interfere, and the stars shine bright and look like they're just above your head. What feels strange is that the constellations in the southern hemisphere are different—there's no Big or Little Dipper.

We spent a day in the rain forest under a beautiful canopy of tropical bushes and trees. Another day we went fishing at the Great Barrier Reef, we but didn't catch anything. We also visited a couple of famous beaches, but didn't get a chance to swim, as they were roped off because of the danger of shark attacks. In the wildlife parks I loved watching ostriches, dingoes and gazelles. Kangaroos stood by the side of the road or walked around oblivious to our presence. We found out that here are more poisonous snakes and spiders in Australia than anywhere else in the world. At one zoo, we got to see a Tiger Snake, the most dangerous snake in the world.

From there we flew to Port Arthur in Tasmania, the site of the famous early 19th-century Australian prison. From 1833 until the 1850s it was the country's largest penal station, housing hardened British and Irish criminals, mostly repeat offenders, as well as juvenile prisoners, boys as young as nine that had been convicted of theft. I had a strange feeling touring what was left of the original buildings. Even eerier was the graveyard on the Isle of the Dead, where prisoners and guards alike were buried on a slope leading down to the ocean. The guards' gravestones were at the top of the hill, and those of the prisoners, lower down by the water.

In an enclosure, I got to see my favorite animal, the Tasmanian Devil, from close up, sleeping no more than 3 feet away from me. They're about the size of a small dog and nasty-looking —big teeth hanging from their muzzles and big pads on their feet —tough little guys. They got their name from the way they howls at night and, we were told, if they took a calf or goat, there'd be nothing left of it in the morning, not a bone. They'll eat anything. I guess I like them because they're tough little characters—that's why I have them on my key bob, the rug mats in my car and little statues out on the pool deck at home.

In a small 4-seat seaplane, we flew below snow-capped mountains into Milford Sound. After we landed, we took a boat ride for a tour and saw seals and many beautiful waterfalls. For many years after Australia had first been discovered, this sound remained unknown because the opening to it can't be seen from the ocean. All the explorers missed it and sailed right by.

We flew on to New Zealand (Donna and must have had 20 different boarding passes on that trip) where there are more sheep than people—80 million! And they have started to raise red deer, as people are beginning to eat more venison than mutton. The inland lodges we stayed at were right where Peter Jackson shot The Lord of the Rings movies—if you build it they will come! Rugged, utterly beautiful mountain country.

In Queensland we visited Cairns, where A.J. Hackett built the first commercial bungee-jumping tower. We declined the offer to take a leap ourselves, but we watched others dive off and plunge toward the large pool below. When you're dangling above the water bouncing gently up and down as if attached to a rubber band, a crew comes out in a little boat to pull you in. One Japanese girl passed out on the way down, and and they had to lift her down while she was still unconscious.

At the airport in Brisbane, Queensland, we visited the dispatch center for American troops and tourists headed to Antarctica. There is a room that can be sealed and temperature controlled to replicate the bitter-cold weather awaiting them. You put on a hat, coat and gloves and go inside. Within minutes, you plunge from 90 degrees outside to 10 below zero while experiencing a snow blizzard. That simulator's main purpose is to train our soldiers who are slated for a tour there what it's like to live in that environment. I'm glad I had the experience, but I was happy to get out and back into the sunshine.

From there we flew back to Hawaii, stayed a couple of days and headed home via Texas. Besides enjoying all the experiences, Donna and I discovered that we were very compatible. We liked the same food and the same activities—fishing, sight-seeing, horseback riding—and we were looking forward to the next big adventure.

The opportunity came in 2007, when Nick and Carole Rinaldi, neighbors of Donna's in Cleveland for 35 years, proposed going on safari in Africa together. We jumped at the suggestion. Once again, the tour was organized by Abercrombie and Kent.

We flew into Nairobi by way of Cairo. From there a small prop plane took us to the Maasai Mara game preserve in Kenya. Open-top Land Rovers took us to our tent city in the bush. There were nine of us. In addition to us couples, there was a family—the parents and their three older sons. Our guide, Pat, was the daughter of the vice president of Kenya. A large woman, she had been educated in the United States, but wore native garb, for the atmosphere, I guess; and she had a wealth of information about the places we visited at her fingertips.

Our tents were spacious and fit for sultans. They had king-sized beds, showers and toilets, rugs on the floor, beautiful bedding and a bar. There was a big dining room tent with pictures on the walls, candelabras on the tables, and fancy place settings. The food was mostly vegetables, all grown in Kenya, bread and soups—the cooks made great soups and baked bread in solar ovens. There was no game, because Kenya does not allow hunting.

The crew would take all of the tents down and transport them to the next place for us while we took our airplanes there.

After breakfast, we'd go out in the Land Rovers into the bush to see animals. We saw water buffalo, giraffes, wildebeests and my favorite—warthogs—and visited a chimpanzee refuge and an orphan elephant camp. Then we'd go back for lunch and head out again for the afternoon.

On the Mara River, our tents were erected in the place where Bill Gates goes every year. The river is famous for its crocodiles and hippopotamuses. More people are killed by hippos in Africa every year than by any other animal, especially when they come ashore. At night we had Maasai warriors standing guard by a fire, watching our tents to make sure the hippos would not come by and trample them. We could hear them fighting by the river. They sounded like big cows.

During the day we went to one of the Maasai villages, where we were greeted by warriors singing to us. The women, heavily adorned, put necklaces on our female adventurers. We men were taken to the main hut where the chief showed us how to build a fire. We learned that they bring their goats and cows into the center of the village every night to protect them from the wild predators in the bush.

Donna and me, and the Maasai warriors that watched out for us at night.

After we returned to Nairobi, we flew back to Cairo. There we visited a factory and witnessed how women made belts and necklaces from beads.

For the next few days, we took a tour into ancient history with an Egyptologist as our guide. The highlight was a trip down the Nile River on a yacht. Only 200 of these special vessels, which sit quite low in the water because they have to go under the bridges, are allowed on the river. On the way we visited Gaza and went inside two of the pyramids. We also looked at the Great Sphinx, whose nose was shot off during World War II when the Nazis used it for target practice. In the Valley of the Kings, we visited the tombs of the pharaohs and rode camels, just like Lawrence of Arabia. We saw a stone quarry where the ancient Egyptians had made obelisks. For me, it was especially interesting to learn how they were able to cut granite without jackhammers, and how they transported the giant stones and stood them upright.

We sailed as far south as Abu Simbel, where engineers had raised the huge statues of Ramses II a hundred feet so they would not be covered by water when the Aswan Dam was built—an astonishing feat. The statues were impressive and made it clear how much the pharaoh was in love with himself.

In Karnak, I bought a rug in honor of Johnny Carson. One of the goofy characters he'd play on *The Tonight Show* was "Karnak the Magnificent," a psychic who wore a big turban and "mysteriously" divined the answers to questions that were handed to him in supposedly sealed envelopes.

Once again, Donna and I had a splendid time, and I would do it again at the drop of a hat.

Since then, we have traveled together twice out West. On our first trip, we visited Jackson Hole, Wyoming, and toured Montana, Oregon and Washington state. In Durango, Colorado, we looked up my friend Matt Zito, and I played in a golf tournament. Later, we headed to San Francisco, where I played golf at Pebble Beach and Spyglass with Donna's son Scott and Kim Marsella. This year we visited Durango again and then headed south to the Grand Canyon, Bryce Canyon and Zion Park, as well as Antelope Canyon, whose stunningly beautiful color strata and cathedral-like walls impressed me most of all. After Chalma,

New Mexico, Taos and Santa Fe, the weather started to get cold, and we headed home.

When not traveling, Donna and I spend a lot of time together. We cook, play rummy, watch TV and enjoy each other's company. I am very happy that she has come into my life!

Donna and me.

Chapter 10
INTO THE FUTURE

After Barbara died, I stayed for two more years in my house in the Bayou on Longboat Key, but it didn't feel right anymore, living there without her. So in 2005, I sold the boat, the skidoos, the '57 Chevy—all the toys—and looked around for another place to live.

I had been playing golf with Dwight Dooley, a realtor I had met on Longboat Key. He was a member of the Laurel Oaks Country Club east of I-75, and we spent a number of pleasant outings there together. I told him that I wanted to move to Sarasota, and he helped me sell my house on Longboat, as well as an investment property I had there. Dwight and his wife, Linda, were very instrumental in helping me find the house I now live in. I liked the golf course at Laurel Oaks, as well as the neighborhoods and community, and when they showed me a place there that had just come on the market, I decided to take a look. I liked what I saw, liked the price and figured it was time to make the move. It didn't hurt that Billy Hoffman already lived there, just a stone's throw away around the corner, just as he did in Scranton when we grew up together there.

The previous owners, Alex and Kathy Hahn, with whom I continue to play golf, had planned to build an addition in back—the architectural plans were drawn up already—and I decided to go ahead and finish it. The wing now houses all the things Barbara loved, including the African masks and jazz musician sculptures we'd collected together.

I've been living there for the last 5 years with Dallas, a 10-year-old West Highland White Terrier. After the many different dogs Barbara and I had, she's probably the last one, the caboose. Dallas likes to bark with excitement at the deer that come to feed in the garden out back. And she is a great companion. When I come home at night, she's always there to greet me, not caring how I smell or look or what time it is.

Sometimes I am amazed how so many of our gang from Petersburg are still around and keep up with one another.

Of course, Billy Hoffman and I remain the closest of friends. Even our dogs get along. He visits Scranton more often than I do, because his mom still lives there. He's invited her to come down here to Sarasota, but she wants to stay up there and be with her friends, whom she has known for 80 years. Billy and I did go to our 50th high school reunion together and had a lot of fun. Besides Betty Gillette, we hooked up with a good half of the old Scranton Tech football team, including our running backs, George Norkaites and Donny Drasba; Tony Russo, a lineman who later had a successful business installing blacktop on highways; and Mike Balcrius, who played offensive and defensive end, was captain of the team our senior year, and later became captain of police in Scranton. It was good to see so many of our former classmates still going strong. We also visited some of the old neighborhoods and hangouts, including Chick's Diner, Texas Wiener and the Minooka Bakery.

We missed Joe Pacifico, who wasn't able to to come. But I had seen him in 2005, when he visited me in Sarasota with his brother Michael. He, Billy Hoffman and I played golf, went out to dinner and spent time together reminiscing. Joe is retired from General Electric. He lives in Arizona now and is still good-looking enough to break someone's heart.

Billy Hoffman, the Reverend Betty Gillette and me at our high school reunion.

As for my family, I haven't seen as much of my brother Bill as I would like to. The main reason is geographic. He lives in Ingram, Texas, now with his second wife, Valerie, whom he met while working in Las Vegas.

Bill has come several times to our hunting camp in Pennsylvania, although he is no longer a member, and he has visited me in Sarasota, too. Last year my brother Butch and I went to Texas to see him. Although the weather was cold and rainy, we didn't let it get in our way and had a splendid time. We played golf, smoked cigars, had some drinks together, and reminisced about the good old days. It was great to see Bill, and I look forward to more such get-togethers with him.

Three brothers: Butch, me and Bill.

Butch and I remain closer at this stage of our lives—both geographically and as far as how often we see each other. He lives in South Carolina now in a townhouse in Myrtle Beach. For many years, he and his friends used to play golf there in the wintertime —it was how they spent their vacation—and he was happy to retire there from his job as a pole man installing lines for Bell Telephone. Although he retired early at 45 (he went for a buyout package he was offered), he continued to consult until a few months ago, traveling all over the United States to teach recent hires how to climb telephone poles.

For a while he was married to a beautiful woman, Judy, whom I still see when I visit New Jersey, and they had two boys—Mike and Charlie Jr., who everyone calls Butchie. Mike works for AT&T and is doing quite well. Butchie is a sales rep for a pharmaceutical company and married an Irish lass, Jannine, who was a police officer in Brooklyn. She now works as a detective for Commissioner Kelly on the anti-terrorist strike force in New York City, and she can tell you a story or two that will make your hair stand on end. They have two young children, Johanna and Matthew, aged 5 and 4 years, respectively.

Jannine and Butchie at her promotion to detective.

My brother Butch is a bachelor now, but he has had a companion for quite some time. Her name is Sharon Dumay, and they are good together. Last summer, I was pleased when they came to Sarasota and watched my house during the two weeks I spent in Jackson Hole, Wyoming.

Butch and I also see each other regularly at our hunting camp in Pennsylvania. It is still one of my favorite places to go, although I make only three or four meetings a year now. In the spring, we all do the things necessary to maintain the camp—mow the grass, do touch-up painting and cut firewood. In the fall, I make sure to spend at least a week there for deer hunting season.

Me and Butch at the hunting camp.

My nephew Butchie, me and my son, Bobby.

We now have 14 members, most of them father-and-son teams. Besides Bobby and me, and Butch and his two sons, there are Donnie Grahamer and his son, Donnie Jr.; Leo Belotti Sr. and Leo Jr.; and Pete Prontitis and his son, Mark. The "single" guys are Bob Karoscik, Larry Defazio (whose daughter was killed on 9-11—she was on the plane from Boston that crashed into the World Trade Center(, and our president, William "Tucker" Frederickson.

*Me and Donnie Grahamer at the hunting camp.
Butch in back, smoking a cigar.*

I love being there with my son, brother and nephews. When it's time for a meeting, I get all pumped up. I fly up early in the week and spend time with friends and family in New Jersey. Then Bobby and I head for the camp. We're there Friday through the following Saturday. During the day, we take walks in the woods, sit in the deer stands waiting for game, and go fishing in the Delaware River. At night, we have a nice supper, play cards, talk, smoke cigars and drink beer. Then we get up the next day and go hunting again. We break camp on Saturday, and I leave to fly back home a day later.

I guess like rugged places. I realized it after my travels to Australia and Africa, but especially after going out West to Colorado and Wyoming. I have come to love that part of the country. I figure, I should have been a cowboy. After spending two weeks last summer in Jackson Hole, I know I like the people out there, and I love seeing wild game—buffalo, antelope, and mule deer. Even the deer in my backyard. No matter how many times I see them, I am in awe of their grace and beauty.

Another outdoor activity I have come to enjoy is golf. Although Donna had never swung a golf club in her life before I met her, I've encouraged her to start playing, too. I bought her a used set of clubs and lessons on various occasions, and she's getting the hang of it and experiencing the joys and frustrations of the game.

I play twice a week now, and take part in tournaments and outings for charity events. I especially enjoy the Special Olympics and have been involved with that organization for several years now. In 2008, Chad Bradski, who was a defensive player for the Indianapolis Colts until two years ago, was our spokesman. He now plays golf here in Sarasota and has become a good friend.

My handicap has come down some since Billy and I won that famous member/member tournament at Gator Creek, but that hasn't made me overconfident or foolhardy. Many players like to bet on games, and I participate, but only small amounts. I was never a high roller, and as in my poker playing days, I don't win a lot and don't lose a lot. Billy, on the other hand, has been in some high-stakes games at Gator Creek. Some of the ex-athletes don't mind throwing money around like it grows on trees. But then, Billy is a very good golfer and can hold his own.

During the winter months when Billy Hoffman lives here, I play golf more often. We go out two to three times a week. We also have supper at each other's houses, cook on the grill, have a few cocktails, smoke cigars, tell stories and, like the ROMEOs, solve the problems of the world. We have never forgotten where we came from. We always tell people that we're from Bunker Hill and Petersburg, the east sections of Scranton. And we tell stories about how we grew up, what our mom and dad did, and how close our families were. While Billy probably became the biggest success from our high school graduating class as far as business is concerned, he never forgot his roots or his friends. I can't say enough good things about him, and I am deeply grateful for the friendship we have had all of our lives.

Me and Shelly.

Four years ago, my daughter, Shelly, and her husband moved down here to Sarasota. Dave has his own business installing and servicing computer systems for local restaurants and other clients. Shelly lives less than three miles away from me, and we see each other often and talk almost every day on the telephone. She still runs the office for our Summit Drilling Company—long distance, via computer—but she leaves the day-to-day work to the staff in New Jersey.

Bobby and me.

My son, Bobby, and I continue to have fun together, fishing and hunting. He consults me from time to time on major decisions that affect our company, but he really is in charge and doing just fine on his own. I always look forward to spending time with him, Debbie and my two grandchildren, Travis and Bradley.

I am delighted that both of my children have turned out well. They have taken many of the things Barbara and I taught them to heart—being helpful to others, treating people the way they would want to be treated, and always doing your best—and are following in our footsteps in putting family life above all else. I am glad that they are proud of their heritage and hold many of the values that are dear to me: honesty, self-reliance, generosity.

I must say that I have had a great life. I have been blessed with good, hard work, a fine and satisfying marriage, two wonderful children and many, many friends. I have done just about everything I wanted to do. I don't have a bucket list. If I died tomorrow, it would be without regrets.

I believe that I am a fortunate man. I am in good health and have enjoyed my retirement. In many ways, I have lived the American Dream. I worked hard and became successful, more successful than I imagined when I started out as a driller (I have lost track how many holes I drilled and how many pumps I have installed, but they must number in the thousands). I am happy that I can say my children are better off financially than I was when I was young, although I wouldn't trade the experiences I had growing up in Scranton for anything in the world.

If I have learned anything in my 70 years, it is never to burn a bridge. If you lose an employee to greener pastures, don't wish them bad luck, but send them off to a brighter future and always keep the door open. You never know what will happen down the road. In the same way, stay as much in touch as you can with your friends and family. They are what make life worth living.

I also believe that you should not look back. If you make a mistake, as we all do, life will go on and will often get better. If I have made any mistakes, they were minor league—like my foolish movie investment—and they didn't end up hurting anyone.

Most of all, as my son said when he delivered Barbara's eulogy, "God only gives you what you can handle."

As I am headed into my eighth decade, my goals for the time I have left are to enjoy life, play golf with my friends, travel and spend time with Donna, hunt and fish, and have good times in my home in Sarasota and out West in Jackson Hole, Wyoming. I look forward to seeing my children, my brothers and many friends, and I'd like to be there when my grandchildren graduate from college

I can't think of anything else for now, but if I do, it will go into my next book.

Shelly and me in front of the house where I grew up on Myrtle Street.

ACKNOWLEDGMENTS

I want to thank my family and friends for their input and knowledge, in particular my son, Bobby, my daughter, Shelly, my brothers, Bill and Butch, and my friend Bill Hoffman.

There are others, too numerous to mention, who provided support and encouragement, but I want to especially thank Donna Dolan for her special role in helping me to keep going with this project.

Several people who read the manuscript and made suggestions and corrections deserve special mention, notably Susan Hicks, Kim Marsella, Linda Robbins and Susan Angermann, who also was instrumental in coming up with the title.

Thomas Mahle of Artful Images helped with the scanning and restoration of the photos in the book.

I want to recognize the gang of golfers that helped me pass the time on Wednesdays and Fridays: Larry Alster, Steve Arnhart, Bill Robbins, Larry Shook, Dwight Dooley, Don Johnstone, Mike Delladonna, Steve Iltis, Paul Parrish, Doug Stevens, Jim Green and Roger Jacobsen.

Also deserving of special thanks are the ROMEOs: Steve Sundheimer, Dave Smith, Jack Feily, John Knowles, Joe Patrick and Phil McGowan.

I have had many friends whose impact on my life has been considerable. If I have left out anyone, please accept my apologies and be sure to let me know—I'll be happy to correct any oversights in subsequent editions.

Finally I want to thank Debbie and Eric at Circle Books on St. Armands for getting me the best editor in the world, Chris Angermann, who brought his expertise and passion for story-telling to this project. Without him, I could not have done it.

INDEX

Abercrombie and Kent, 129, 132
Abu Simbel, Egypt, 135
Acker Drilling, 83
Adams, Greg, *92*, 98, 102, 109
Adams, Mary Beth, 98, 109, *109*
Aizinger, Paul, 116
Allmand Brothers, 117
Andrea Doria, 49
Antelope Canyon, 135
April Well and Pump Company, 83
Armonk, New York, 82
Arnold, Eddie, 111
Assanti, Mike, 85, 86
Assanti, Lenny, 85, 86
Aswan Dam, Egypt, 135
AT&T, 90, 141
Attica Prison, 72
Australia, 129-132
Autry, Gene, 25
Ayer's Rock, 130
Balcrius Mike, 138
Bamboo Homes, 108
Banner Homes, 71, 72
Barbutti, Pete, 17
Barr, Edith, 111
Bayou, the, Longboat Key, 108, 110, 119, 123, 137
Bedminster, New Jersey, 94
Bell Telephone (New Jersey Bell), 77, 90, 140
Bell Theater, 24-25
Belotti, Leo Jr., 143
Belotti, Leo Sr., 143
Bent Tree Golf Course, 112

Beppler, Earl, 70
Berwick, Pennsylvania, 6, 41
Betti, Diane, 41
Betti, Nick, 41
Betts, Dicky, 117
Bidabadi, Dr. Homayoun, 121
Biden, Joe, 3
Bitterman, Stuart, 123
Boston Red Sox, 117
Bradski, Chad (*Indianapolis Colts*), 144
Bridgewater, New Jersey, 71, 84, 86, 91, 98
Brisbane, Queensland
Bronson, Billy, 16
Bronx, New York, 77
Bryce Canyon, 135
Bucky, Mr., 36
Buccaneer, the, 110
Bunker Hill, 13, 18, 32, 71, 145
Burshel Dairy, 7
Buttonwood Harbor, Sarasota Bay, 120, 122
Café L'Europe, 105
Cairns, Queensland, 132
Cairo, Egypt, 133, 134
Carbondale, 3
Carlisimo Sr., Pete, 68
Carson, Johnny (*The Tonight Show*), 17, 135
Cassidy, Hopalong, 25
Castelano, Carmen, 16
Cerato, Mr., 31
Central High School, 15, 30, 40
Chalma, New Mexico, 135

INDEX

Chapin, Harry, 69
Chick's Diner, 35, 57, 138
Chico, 57-58
Clarks Summit, Pennsylvania, 28, 83, 84
Cleaves, Dick, 83, 84
Coca Cola Company, 72, 73
Cohen, Mike, 127, 128
Collins, Jeff, 125
Columbia Restaurant, 105
Community Medical Center, 4
Co-Op City, Bronx, New York, 77-78
Cortese family, 9
Dallas, West Highland White Terrier, *122*, 138
Davis, Kenny (Buddy), 41, 43
Defazio, Larry, 83, 143
Delaware Lackawanna and Western Railroad, 4
Delaware River, 9, 99, 101, 109, 143
Detroit Tigers, 6, 57
Dolan, Donna, 107, 128, 129-136, *134, 136*, 144, 147
Dolan, Jack, 129
Dolan, Heidi, 129
Dolan, Scott, 129, 135
Dolan Tim, 129
Don Juan Wines, 58, *59,* 68
Dooley, Dwight, 137
Dooley, Linda, 137
Doty, Carl, 127, 128
Doylestown, Pennsylvania, 94
Drasba, Donny, 138
Dumay, Sharon, 141
Dunmore, 3, 7, 11, 14, 32
Durango, Colorado, 123, 135
East River, New York, 74
East Scranton, 3, 31
East Scranton Sportsmen's Club (hunting camp), 9, 57, 76, 83, 113, 119, 139, 142-143
East Stroudsburg University, 25
Erie Pennsylvania Railroad, 3, 7, 11, 82
Everhart Museum of Natural History,

Science and Art, 17
Fachetti's Tavern, 37
Fall River, Massachusetts, 49
Feetzer, Dick, Bridgewater Chief of Police, 87
Feily, Jack, 117
Finderne Heights, New Jersey, 84
Fisk, Carlton (*Boston Red Sox*), 117
Flemington, New Jersey, 102
Flood of 1955, 36-40
Fortune Magazine, 73
Foytack, Joe, 18
Foytack, Paul, 16, 57
Frederickson, William "Tucker," 143
Freedom Land, 77
Frontier/Kemper, 113
Fulton Fish Market, Manhattan, 73-75
Garner, James, 67
Gates, Bill, 133
Gator Creek Golf Club, 116, 126, 144
Gavazzi Tire Company, 72, 90
Gaza, Egypt, 134-135
Gertrude Hawk Chocolates, 32
Giles Drilling Company, 43, 55, 69, 70, 71, 78
Gillette, Reverend Betty, 42, 138, *139*
Glacier Bay Park, Alaska, 114
Globe, 57
Godfrey, Arthur, 64
Goethals Bridge, 82
Grahamer, Don, 41, 47, 49-54, *52, 53,* 57, 64-66, 69, 77, 80-81, *80,* 93, 96, 97, 99, 143, *143*
Grahamer, Don, Jr., 57, 70, 143
Grahamer, Gail, 70
Grahamer, Helen, 66, 70, 99
Grahamer, Holly, 70
Graig, Cynthia, 121
Grand Canyon, 135
Great Barrier Reef, Australia, 130
Gregory, Frank, 46
Hackett, A.J., 132
Hahn, Alex, 138

INDEX

Hahn, Kathy, 138
Hahnemann Hospital, 4, 59
Haller Testing Laboratory, 73, 74, 75, 83
Hanlon, James T., 38
Harvey, Bob, 23, 24
Hawk, Elmer, 25, 32
Hawk, Gertrude, 32
Hawkins, Freddy, 64
Hess Oil, 97
Highfield, Ellen, 37-38
Highfield, Elliott, 37-38
Hill, Billy, 16
Hillsborough, New Jersey, 72, 73
Hoffman, Bill, 14-15, *16*, 18, 19, 20, 25, 30, 33, 35, 36, *36*, 37, 39, 40, 41, 58, 61, 62, 72, 73, 81, 107, 111, 117, 126, *126*, 127, 128, 137, 138, 139, *139*, 44, 145
Hoffman, Harry, 14, 25
Hoffman, Sue, 14, 31
Hoffman, Mickey, 72, 107
Holder (grandfather), *29*
Howard, Mr., 20-21
Houston, Whitney, 123
Howell, Dyke, 113-115, 117
Huckleberry Mary, 13
Hudson River, New York, 46, 63, 81
Hudson River Parkway, New York, 77
Hunting Camp (see East Scranton Sportsman's Hunting Club)
Hurricane Diana, 36
Hurricane Donna, 54
Incheon Harbor, Korea, 27
Indiana University of Pennsylvania, 15, 41
Interstate 287, 79
Jackson, Happy, 41, 82
Jackson, Samuel, 112
Jackson Hole, Wyoming, 135, 141, 144, 147
Karampolis, Mr., 35
Karnak, Egypt, 135
Karoscik, Bob, 143
Kelly, Jack, 67

Kelly, Police Commissioner of New York, 141
Kenya, 133-134
Klassner, Frank, 41, 43, 47, 49-54, *51, 52, 53*
Knauer, Judy, 25
Knight, Ray, 112
Knowles, John, 117, 121
Korea, 25-28
Kreilick, Bob, *7, 11, 16, 23, 40, 53, 56, 59, 62, 76, 80, 109, 116, 118, 124, 125, 126, 134, 136, 139, 140, 142, 143, 145, 146*, 148
   Alligator hunting, 115-116
   "Crick," nickname, 25, 42
   Drilling Jobs
      Lake Placid, New York, 64-66
      Newark Airport, 81
      Texas Tower, 47-54
      Co-Op City, 77-78
      Stewart Air Force Base, 81
      Verrazano Bridge, 63-64
      Washington Metro, 78
      World Trade Center, 73-76
   Grade School years, 20-25
   Golfing, 11-12, 116-117, 126-128, 44
   Fishing, 106, 114, 123-125
   High School years, 30-42
   Hunting, 113-114, 142-143
   Meeting and marrying Barbara, 60-63
   Meeting Donna Dolan, 128-129
   Retirement, 105-148
   Summit Well and Pump Company, 84-92, 95
   Trip to Africa, 132-135
   Trip to Australia and New Zealand, 129-132
Kreilick, Barbara, *v*, 1, 59-63, *62*, 65-66, 67, 68-70, 72, 82, 83, 86, 87, 90, *92*, 96, 99, 100, *101*, 103, 105, 108, 109-113, *109, 110*, 119-122, *122*, 123, 37, 138, 146, 147

INDEX

Kreilick, Bill, 4, *7, 10, 11,* 12, 17, 21-22, 25-28, *23, 26, 28, 29,* 39, 41, 63, 76, *76,* 90, 118, *118,* 139, 140, *140*
Kreilick, Bobby, 19, 64, 69, 70, 72, 73, 82, 85, 86, 87, 91, 92, *92,* 96, 98, 99, 101, 102, 103, *104,* 106, 107, 110, *110,* 111, 119, 120, 124, *124,* 125, 126, *142,* 146, *146,* 147
Kreilick, Bradley, 102, 103-104, *104,* 146
Kreilick, Charles (Butch), 4, 8, 12, 21-24, *23,* 63, *76,* 77, 82, 90, 92, 139, 140, *140,* 142, *142,* 143, *143*
Kreilick, Charles (grandfather), *29*
Kreilick, Charlie Jr. (Butchie), 141, *141, 142,* 143
Kreilick, Debbie, 87, 102, 103, *104,* 110, 111, 120, 146
Kreilick, Janet, 5, 93
Kreilick, Jannine, 141, *141*
Kreilick, Johanna, 141
Kreilick, Matthew, 141
Kreilick, Judy, 141
Kreilick, Ray, *5, 7,* 5-11, *11,* 13, 19, *20,* 21, 22, 25, 26, *28, 29,* 31, 33, 34, 58, 63, 73, *76,* 75-76, 82, 93, *94*
Kreilick, Ruth, 14, 62
Kreilick, Margaret, *7, 9, 10, 11, 12,* 12-13, 21, 22, 25, *28,* 33, 34, 59-60, 63, 93, 94, *94*
Kreilick, Mike, 141, 143
Kreilick, Michelle (Shelly), see Smith, Shelly
Kreilick, Travis, 66, 102, 103, *103, 104,* 146
Kreilick, Valerie, 139
Lackawanna River Valley, 3, 36, 39
Lake Elko, 102
Lake Lincoln, 17, 2
Lake Placid, New York, 64-66
Lake Scranton, 69
Lake Wallenpaupack, 21, 61
Lake Okeechobee, 115
Largo, Florida, 120

Laurel Oaks Country Club, 128, 137
Levallier, Mike (*Pittsburgh Pirates*), 117
Lido Key, Florida, 107
Little Rock Glen, 18
Longboat Key, Florida, 105, 107, 110, 137
Longboat Key Club, 111, 112, 123
Longboat Mooring Marina, 108, 109
Lopez, Nancy, 112
The Lord of the Rings movies, 132
Lycoming College, 24
Maasai Mara game preserve, Kenya, 133
Maggie Valley, North Carolina, 107
Magnotta, Will, 15
Magnotta Bar, 31
Mara River, Kenya, 133
Marsella, Kim, 129, 135
Massai, 133-134
Martell, Brian, Captain, 103
Mantle, Mickey, 26
Maywood College, 14
McFadden, Dan, 113-115
McGowan, Phil, 117
McInaw, Pat, 99
Mealy, Alexandra (Alex), 33, 93
Milford Sound, Australia, 131
Minooka Bakery, 68, 138
Montana, Joe, 107
Montgomery, Albert, 33, *33*
Montgomery, Janet, 33, *33,* 93
Moseley, Foster, 86
Mostie, 18-19
Mote Marine Laboratory, 108, 122
Muehlenberg School #5, 15, 31
Murphy, Mr., 30
Myrtle Street Methodist Church, 33, 42
Nairobi, Kenya, 133, 134
Nantucket Shoals, 48, 54
Nay Aug Park, 17, 18, 20, 35
Nay Aug Park Zoo, 17, 58
Newark Airport, 81
New Zealand, 131-132
Neisler, Chris, 119

INDEX

Nickelson, Walter, 27
Nile River, 134
Norkaites, George, 138
Norfolk Naval Ship Yards, 81
Norfolk Portsmouth Bridge Tunnel, 55
Notre Dame University, 107
"The Office" (television show), 3
Olmsted, Frederick Law, 17
Olmsted Air Force Base, 38
O'Neill, Joe (see Joe Foytack), 18
Pacifico, Joe, 15, *16,* 35, 36, *36,* 37, 41, 61, 139
Pacifico, Michael, 37, 139
Parris Island, South Carolina, 25
Patrick, Joe, 117
Patrick's Restaurant, 117
Paul Smith's College, 66
Payton, Walter, 105
Peggy (cousin), 33
Pensacola, Florida, 28
Petersburg, 3, 13, 32, 38, 145
Petersburg Blue Devils, 58
    Petersburg Silk Mill, 3, 4, 14, 17, 24, 35, 61
Pike County, 9, 57
Piscataway, New Jersey, 79, 86
Pittston, 3
Plainfield, New Jersey, 73
Port Arthur, Tasmania, 131
Poseidon, the, 111
Possumtown, New Jersey, 85
Prince, 32
Princeton, New Jersey, 72
Princeton University, 98
Prontitis, Mark, 143
Prontitis, Pete, 143
Raritan Canal, 79
Red Bank, New Jersey, 70
Red Raiders, 35
Reliable Drilling, 77
Rinaldi, Carole, 132
Rinaldi, Nick, 132
Ritchie, Bobby, 41

Ritchie, Tom, 41, 82
Rizzo, Mrs. (famous pizza), 13
Roaring Brook, 15, 18, 35, 36, 37
Roberts, Gary, 108
Robinson, Don, *(LA Dodgers)* 117
Rodgers, Roy, 25
ROMEOS, 117, 121, 145
Rozelle, Casey, 107
Rozelle, Cubby, 34
Rozelle, Gail, 17
Rozelle, JoAnn, 17
Rozelle, Jan, 91, 107
Rozelle, Ken, 17, 58, 61, 90-92, *91,* 96, 107
Rozelle, Pete, 92
Rozelle, Renee, 107
Russo, Tony, 138
Saint Mary's Church, 63
Sanford, Florida, 33
Santa Fe, New Mexico, 136
Saranac Lake, New York, 64
Sarasota, Florida, 15, 95, 102, 105, 107, 11, 119, 120, 137, 138, 139, 141, 144, 145, 147
Sarasota Bay, 108, 120
Savage, Chuck, 108
Scanlon, Grandma, *26*
Schenkel's, 111
Schmidt, Donnie, 8-9
Schmidt, Harold, 8
Scotch Plains, New Jersey, 70
Scranton, Pennsylvania, 3, 4, 7, 11, 14, 15, 18, 19, 21, 24, 27, 33, 34, 36, 38, 39, 40, 54, 57, 62, 64, 66, 67, 69, 71, 72, 82, 84, 90, 91, 93, 137, 138, 145, 147
    1955 Flood, 36-39
    Adams Avenue, 30
    Ash Street, 14, 31, 36, 37
    Cedar Avenue, 60
    Gibson Street, 30
    James Street, 3, 14, 17
    Lackawanna Avenue, 35
    Matthew Avenue, 13, 32

INDEX

Moosic Street, 35, 69
Mulberry Street, 24
Myrtle Street, 3, *26,* 32
Prescott Avenue, 24
Richter Avenue, 15, 35, 37
Union Avenue, 37
Wheeler Avenue, 3, 31
Scranton Tech High School, 15, 17, 30, 34, 41, 138
Scranton University, 35, 68
The Scranton Times, 14, 27, 30, 38
The Scranton Tribune, 30
Sea Ray Sun Dancer, *Summit,* 105
Seagrave, Bill, 119, 120
Seagrave, Lena, 119, 120
Seton Hall, 68, 98
Shannon, Beverly, 111
Shannon, Ralph, 111
Sidney, Australia, 129
Skidaway Island, Georgia, 107
Sliwa, Henry, 84, 85, 86, 89-90, 95, 96, 106-107
Sliwa, Marie, 84, 90, 106-107
Smith, Dave, retired Delta pilot, 117
Smith, Dave, married to Shelly Smith, 95, 107, *118,* 120, 145
Smith, Jenna, 119
Smith, Jeremy, 119
Smith, Johnelle, 119, 128
Smith, Pal, 119
Smith, Shelly (Michelle Kreilick), 65, 66, 67-68, 70, 71-72, 82, 86, 87, 91, *92,* 93, 94, 95, 100, 102, 107, *118,* 120, 128, 145, *145, 148*
South Catholic High School, 59
South Scranton, 38, *39,* 60, 63, 66
Special Olympics, 144
St. Armands Circle, 105, 107, 128
Steward Air Force Base, 81
Stockholm, 49
Sullivan, Ed (Ed Sullivan Show), 17
Summit Drilling Company, Inc., 97, 98, 102, 119, 146

Summit Well and Pump Company, 84, 85, 91, 95, 99
Sumski, Albina, 60, 67-68, *67*
Sumski, Bartholomew (Bart), 60, 67, *67*
Sumski, Dolores, 63
Sumski, Joe, 63
Sumski, Lorraine, 63
Sundheimer, Lori, 120, 121
Sundheimer, Steve, 117, 120, 121, 125
Taylor, Jim (*Green Bay Packers*), 26
Texas Tower, 47-54, 48, *49, 50, 53,* 55
Texas Wiener, 35, 138
"30,000 Pounds of Bananas", 69
Timlan, Father, 61, 62
The Tonight Show, 135
Trans-Hudson Tunnel, 99
Tri-State Area, 56
Trunzo, Pat, *36*
Tupper Lake, New York, 64
University of Rhode Island, 95, 98
Verrazano Narrows Bridge, 63
"Verities & Balderdash," 69
Virginia Tech University, 107
Wall Street, New York City, 74
Warren George Drilling Company, 46
Washington Metro, 78, 81
Wayne, John, 25
Webber, Emmitt, 108
Webe, Linda, 108
Weiss, Charlie, 24
Westminster Presbyterian Church, 33
White, Randy Wayne, 106,
Wilkes-Barre, 3, 4
William Prescott Elementary School, 15, *16,* 20, 41
Wilson, Kendal, 115, *116*
Winters, Spike, 10
Whiteface Mountain, 65, 66
Wojdak, Steve, 15, *16,* 20, 30, *36,* 40, 41, 61, 62
Woods, Tiger, 112
World Trade Center, 73-75, 121, 143
Zito, Carol, 123

INDEX

Zito, Glen, 123, 124
Zito, Jeff, 123
Zito, Matt, 123, 124, 125, 135
Zion National Park, 135